Russian Propaganda Hits Its Mark

Experimentally Testing the Impact of Russian Propaganda and Counter-Interventions

TODD C. HELMUS, JAMES V. MARRONE,
MAREK N. POSARD, DANIELLE SCHLANG

Sponsored by the California Governor's
Office of Emergency Services

RAND NATIONAL SECURITY RESEARCH DIVISION

For more information on this publication, visit www.rand.org/t/RRA704-3

Library of Congress Cataloging-in-Publication Data is available for this publication.
ISBN: 978-1-9774-0594-4

Published by the RAND Corporation, Santa Monica, Calif.

Cover images: guteksk7/Adobe Stock; iiierlok_xolms/Adobe Stock; carmelod/Adobe Stock; FishPouch/Adobe Stock

Preface

Given the size and scope of the Russian propaganda campaign that targeted the U.S. electorate in 2016, it is critical to understand both the impact of that campaign and the mechanisms that can reduce the impact of future campaigns. To assess this, we recruited a large sample of participants on Facebook and asked them to view and rate Russian propaganda memes, real news headlines, and false news headlines. We also tested how two different types of interventions—media literacy content and revealing the source of the content—attenuate audience reactions. In this report we detail the research design and findings and offer recommendations for policy and future research. In accordance with the appropriate statutes and regulations regarding human subject protection, the researchers used human subject protection protocols for this report and its underlying research.

This report is the third in a four-part series of analyses conducted by RAND Corporation researchers for the California Governor's Office of Emergency Services (Cal OES) and intended to help policymakers and the public understand—and mitigate—the threat of online foreign interference in national, state, and local elections.

This research was sponsored by Cal OES and conducted within the International Security and Defense Policy Center of the RAND National Security Research Division (NSRD). NSRD conducts research and analysis for the Office of the Secretary of Defense, the U.S. Intelligence Community, U.S. State Department, allied foreign governments, and foundations.

For more information on the RAND International Security and Defense Policy Center, see www.rand.org/nsrd/isdp or contact the director (contact information is provided on the webpage).

Contents

Boxes, Figures, and Tables

Boxes

Figures

Tables

Summary

Since the 2016 presidential election (and possibly before that), Russia has attempted to influence Americans through propaganda efforts on social media—and likely will continue to do so. Although our research cannot speak to the impact of Russian propaganda on society at large, we do identify that Russian propaganda successfully elicits strong reactions in the very audiences that it targets.

In our study, we used actual Russian propaganda in a randomized controlled trial to determine how people reacted emotionally to the content, whether they would "like" or share it,[1] and whether there are ways to help people recognize propaganda and keep them from spreading it.

How the Experiment Was Conducted

To study the effect of various propaganda interventions, we used a randomized controlled trial with four treatment conditions. We recruited more than 1,500 participants on Facebook and asked them (1) to rate various pieces of social media content (memes)[2] in terms of how the

[1] We have put "like" in quotation marks where we are referring to publicly indicating approval by clicking an icon. We have done this to differentiate between this action and simply having a favorable feeling toward something.

[2] A *meme*, as originally defined by evolutionary biologist Richard Dawkins, 1976, referred to a behavior or style that spread from person to person. It has since been redefined, according to McCrae, 2017, as "any fad, joke or memorable piece of content that spreads virally across the web, usually in the form of short videos or photography accompanied by a clever caption."

content made them feel and (2) whether they would "like" or share what they had seen. Participants were also asked questions about their political beliefs, where they get their news, and their susceptibility to falsehoods.

The participants were then randomly assigned to one of four groups:

1. a control group that received no intervention
2. a group that saw labels on social media content revealing that Russia is the source
3. a group that viewed a video about media literacy
4. a group that viewed memes about media literacy.

Participants first viewed either placebo pretest content or their assigned media literacy interventions. They were then shown and asked to rate propaganda memes that Russia used during the 2016 election; they were also shown ads or images with false news headlines, real news headlines, and public service announcements. Participants in the second group saw labels alongside this propaganda that revealed its source; participants in the other groups were blind to the source.

Findings

Our findings indicate that Russian content is particularly effective at achieving its goal of generating strong reactions along partisan lines, engendering stronger emotional responses than those brought on by real or false news and creating a starker partisan divide. Also of concern: Strongly positive emotional reactions to such social media content increase the chances that participants will self-report "liking" and sharing it. These findings appear to be in line with our understanding of Russian goals and objectives for propaganda: to elicit strong reactions in partisans that, in turn, can facilitate the spread and potential influence of manipulated content.

We also found that revealing the source of the Russian memes reduced the probability of a positive emotional response to content that aligned with a participant's ideology. Compared with the emotional effects generated among participants for whom the source was hidden, participant willingness to engage with the content on Facebook by "liking" or sharing material for which the source was exposed was weaker. In the overall sample, revealing the source reduced the likelihood that participants would "like" pro-U.S. Russian content, but no other effects for "liking" or sharing were statistically significant.

We found that revealing the source and showing a video about media literacy had a stronger impact for a unique subset of participants defined by news consumption habits. We created audience typologies based on the sources of news they read. Two particular audience profiles stood out: a group we call *Partisan Left*, who lean left politically and among whom the *New York Times* was the most-cited news source; and a group we call *Partisan Right*, who lean right politically and who get their news from Fox News or from politically far-right outlets. Participants in both of these groups exhibit strong responses to Russian memes that align with their political ideologies, and both groups demonstrated a reduced emotional response to that propaganda and were less likely to "like" that propaganda when informed of its Russian source. The video on media literacy also appeared to reduce the number of self-reported "likes" for pro-U.S. and politically right-leaning Russian content in the *Partisan Right* subgroup. Participants in either of these subgroups might represent an ideal audience for future intervention efforts.

Conclusions and Implications for Future Research

Our main findings suggest that Russian content produces strong emotional reactions and that the very partisans it is targeting "like" and share the content at higher rates than other consumers of social media. These results are problematic because of the potential scope of a Russian propaganda campaign on social media. If state-sponsored propaganda content is quickly detected and immediately removed from the networks of social media platforms, then these results might have limited utility—there is no point in warning people about content that is already inaccessible. But if administrators are slow to remove such content, or if academic researchers outpace the platforms in detecting state-sponsored campaigns, then plug-ins of the type used to notify consumers of Twitter bots might be valuable.

Although our work was exploratory in nature, the subgroupings we defined by news consumption might identify audiences for which counter-Russian propaganda interventions might yield the most promise. The media literacy interventions produced inconsistent effects overall, but those who viewed the video on media literacy self-reported fewer "likes" for Russian right-leaning and pro-U.S. content.

Acknowledgements

We are grateful to the numerous individuals who supported the conduct of this research. In particular, we thank our sponsors at the California Governor's Office of Emergency Services. We are also grateful to the staff at IREX, particularly Matthew Vanderwerff. We are especially grateful to Melissa Bauman, whose dedicated work greatly improved the prose of this report. We also owe enormous credit to our colleagues at the RAND Corporation's Survey Research Group. Without their dedicated work, this survey experiment would not have been possible. Finally, we are grateful to Luke Matthews and Alice Huguet at RAND for their considered and thoughtful reviews. All errors are the sole responsibility of the authors.

Abbreviations

ABC	American Broadcasting Company
ABIC	adjusted BIC
BIC	Bayesian Information Criterion
CAIC	asymptotically consistent Akaike Information Criterion
Cal OES	California Governor's Office of Emergency Services
COVID-19	coronavirus disease 2019
CRT	Cognitive Reflection Test
LCA	latent class analysis
NBC	National Broadcasting Company
NES	National Election Studies
NPR	National Public Radio
PSA	Public Service Announcement

CHAPTER ONE

Introduction

Since the 2016 presidential election (and possibly before that), Russia has attempted to influence Americans through propaganda efforts on social media—and likely will continue to do so. This report adds to a small but growing body of literature that attempts to determine whether Russia's attempts to influence Americans through social media campaigns actually work. The answer, based on our study results, is yes.

Our findings indicate that Russian propaganda efforts trigger strong emotions that could work to intensify political divisions in the United States. To counter this, we examined several ways to protect social media users against Russian propaganda. Our study is unique in several ways. It is one of the first to show that Russian propaganda content works, in part, by eliciting positive emotions that could exacerbate political divisions in American society. Our study also appears to be the first to use actual Russian propaganda in a randomized controlled trial investigating possible methods to curtail misinformation efforts.

This report is the third in a four-part series of analyses conducted by the RAND Corporation's National Security Research Division for the California Governor's Office of Emergency Services and intended to help policymakers and the public understand—and mitigate—the threat of online foreign interference in national, state, and local elections (Figure 1.1). The first report summarized what existing research says about foreign information efforts (Posard et al., 2020). The second report documented the existence of what appeared to be state-sponsored accounts on Twitter seeking to influence U.S. attitudes toward the 2020 presidential election (Marcellino et al.,

Figure 1.1
What This Series Covers

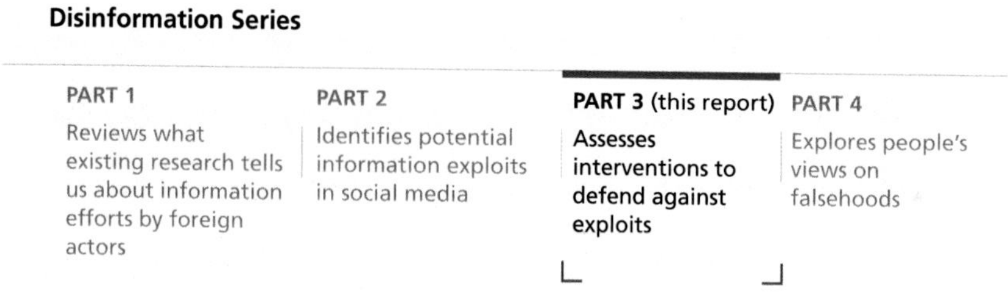

2020). These state-sponsored accounts bear the hallmark attributes of Russian propaganda.

In this report, we describe a rigorous experiment that we conducted to assess (1) how audiences react to Russian propaganda content and (2) several potential interventions for their mitigating effects on positive reactions to propaganda. In Chapter Two, we examine the rationale for this study and review some of the relevant background literature. In Chapter Three, we summarize the methods used in this experimental design. We present the results in Chapter Four, and we summarize the findings and address our conclusions in Chapter Five.

The final report in this series will analyze qualitative interviews conducted with survey respondents to better understand their views on falsehoods.

CHAPTER TWO

Russian Propaganda, Political Memes, and Fissures in American Society

One major goal of Russia's social media–based propaganda campaign targeting the 2016 election was to polarize and disrupt societal cohesion by exacerbating partisan divisions. This was the conclusion of the first report in this series, which noted that "Russia seeks to manipulate important and divisive social and political issues as a way to alter public opinion, create and exacerbate fissures, and disrupt political processes" (Posard et al., 2020, p. 5). This assessment is supported by an assessment of reflexive control theory, which is a theoretical research program developed by Vladimir Lefebvre and others that first appeared in Soviet military literature in the 1960s (Lefebvre, 1966). The model rests on the tenet that people live in a polarized world of cooperation versus conflict, and it would predict that Russia would use propaganda as a means to trigger reactions that drive people to ideological extremes, making it nearly impossible to build a consensus. (See Thomas, 2004; Chotikul, 1986; and Radin, Demus, and Marcinek, 2020.)

The classic political meme is a favorite Russian tool. A *meme*, as originally defined by evolutionary biologist Richard Dawkins, 1976, referred to a behavior or style that spread from person to person. It has since been redefined, according to McCrae, 2017, as "any fad, joke or memorable piece of content that spreads virally across the web, usually in the form of short videos or photography accompanied by a clever caption." Memes (Box 2.1), in the words of one report on Russian disinformation, "turn big ideas into emotionally resonant snippets" and represent the "propaganda of the digital age" (DiResta et al., 2019).

Numerous studies describe how Russia targeted U.S. audiences with highly politicized memes. Alvarez, Choi, and Strover, 2020, high-

> **Box 2.1**
>
> **A Favorite Russian Tool**
>
> Memes, in the words of one report on Russian disinformation, "turn big ideas into emotionally resonant snippets" and represent the "propaganda of the digital age."

lighted how Russia incorporated emotional appeals into Facebook ads focusing on divisive U.S. topics, such as race, police brutality, nationalism, immigration, and gun rights. Hugh and Pechenkina analyzed the content of influential Russian propagandist accounts and observed that Russian content went viral as a result of "overwhelming negative, politicized messaging on the right, yet apolitical, identity affirming messages on the left" (Hugh and Pechenkina, 2020, abstract). Linvill et al., 2019, documented how right-leaning Russian trolls broadcast nativist and right-leaning populist messages, and left-leaning trolls sent liberal messages often focused on cultural identity.[1]

The divisiveness of Russian propaganda was further established by Ribeiro et al., 2019, who used U.S. Census-representative surveys to test audience perceptions of Facebook ads employed by Russia as part of its propaganda campaign. That study indicated that political partisans were more likely than the sample as a whole to approve of the advertisements that were in agreement with their attitudes. Partisans were also less likely than the sample as a whole to believe that attitude-congruent ads contained a "false claim."[2]

Although some have described Russian propaganda as "fake news," the political memes that Russia has disseminated often do not purport to be "true" and do not present falsifiable statements (Alvarez,

---

[1] In addition, Stewart, Arif, and Starbird, 2018, analyzed how Russian troll accounts retweeted content related to the #BlackLivesMatter movement and found that the accounts "took advantage of" the political divisions surrounding that movement.

[2] Ribeiro et al., 2019, also examined the click-through rate of the advertisements, a ratio of the number of users who clicked on the advertisement over the total number that saw the ad in their news feed. The researchers found an average click-through rate of 10.8 percent, which is far higher than the average rate for Facebook ads across all industries, which is 0.9 percent.

Choi, and Strover, 2020).[3] We provide examples in Appendix A demonstrating that some Russian content does not even state an explicit opinion with which a viewer could agree or disagree. Along politically right-leaning lines, an image of Jesus is captioned, "Like if you believe, keep scrolling if you don't." On the politically left-leaning side, an image of a Black voter is captioned, "I won't vote. Will you?"

This poses a unique challenge in creating interventions that are designed to limit the influence of Russian propaganda. Such interventions as issuing corrections or fact-checking do not apply to this breed of Russian propaganda content. That the memes present emotionally excitable content to partisan audiences who might be more incited to share it further hamstrings protective measures.

Two Types of Interventions: Revealing the Source and Media Literacy Education

In our study, we examined two unique mechanisms that might be able to undercut the impact of Russian propaganda content. First, we examined the impact of exposing participants to two forms of low-cost and scalable media literacy campaigns: (1) a 97-second video designed to improve media literacy and (2) specially tailored educational memes that in part sought to help audiences be more critical about the sources of content and the unwritten purpose of the content they see. Although the video and memes offered only small levels of exposure to media literacy content, we found it conceivable that such warnings might make participants reconsider the intent of the source or the risks of sharing the content, blunting the audience's responses to the propaganda content. Prior research has demonstrated that diverse media literacy interventions can have moderate and positive impacts in improving participants' beliefs, attitudes, and behaviors related to media (Jeong,

[3] Propaganda is often classified using such terms as *malinformation* (e.g., leaked documents), *misinformation* (e.g., misleading content that includes half-truths), and *disinformation* (e.g., complete falsehoods, such as forgeries or fictitious declarative statements). The use of political memes that bear no falsifiable information consequently appears to be a gray area among the various degrees of falsehoods.

Cho, and Hwang, 2012). More pertinent to our work, another study (Guess et al., 2020) found that a Facebook-based media literacy campaign improved discernment between real and false news headlines. (We are unaware of any prior studies specifically examining the impact of media literacy content on individuals' responses to Russian propaganda political memes.)

Second, we tested the impact of directly revealing the malign source of the propaganda content. In the case of Russian content, we provided a simple statement under the meme that the source of the meme was the "Russian government" and that it was disseminated as part of a "covert propaganda campaign in the United States." Our view was that offering such source information represented what might be considered the strongest intervention designed to undercut audience faith in the content. Given that much of the Russian content cannot be disputed based on accuracy or falsehood, informing audiences that the content is propagandist in nature and authored by a major U.S. adversary should, in theory, deflate audience reaction to the content. We can assume that offering such source information is akin to interventions that use warning labels or labels calling out the headlines of news stories that have been disputed by third-party fact-checkers, which prior research has shown leads to a modest reduction in the perceived accuracy of headlines (Pennycook et al., 2020). However, this outcome could be in doubt for partisan audiences that are inclined to strongly relate to partisan content.

The Degree to Which Russian Content Elicits a Positive Emotional Reaction and Is "Liked" and Shared

Our study also afforded an opportunity to test the efficacy of Russian propaganda, which numerous others have declared is a critical need (Box 2.2). As noted, Ribeiro et al., 2019, examined the degree to which partisan audiences agreed with Russian content and the degree to which they believed the content contained a false claim. They also tested whether audiences would report the ad to Facebook for violations of terms of service. In lieu of these measures, we asked participants to

> **Box 2.2**
>
> **A Unique Opportunity**
>
> We examined two unique mechanisms that might be able to undercut the impact of Russian propaganda content.

rate the degree to which they would "like" or share the content with their Facebook networks.[4] We also assessed the degree to which the content elicited a positive emotional reaction.

Why assess the emotional reaction of the content? Several strands of research suggest that emotional reactions are a critical pathway by which to affect consumer behaviors toward propaganda. The dual-processing model of persuasion, for example, highlights that persuasion can occur through two channels. The first is referred to as the *central* or *direct route* and requires effortful and deliberate consideration of an argument's merits. The second is referred to as the *peripheral* or *heuristic route*, requires fewer resources, and is less analytical (Xu, 2017). In a summary of the theory and research, Alvarez et al., 2020, notes that the latter "heuristic process" relies on such accessible information as "source identity and status or cues that quickly elicit affective associations." The authors continue to note that "meme-like qualities and brevity associated with Facebook posts, particularly with image-based posts, are amenable to such processing."

Evidence suggests that this emotion-arousing content is particularly influential. In a summary of available evidence, one research team concluded that research "suggests that emotionally charged messages have a higher probability of becoming viral" and that certain emotions can enhance a message's credibility (Tucker et al., 2018, p. 44). Accordingly, research has shown that emotionally positive content spreads faster through online channels (Berger and Milkman, 2012) and that audiences are more likely to share or interact with emotionally charged social media posts. Alvarez et al., 2019, analyzed the sentiment of Russian Facebook advertisements and found that the positivity of ads was

4 We have put "like" in quotation marks where we are referring to publicly indicating approval by clicking an icon. We have done this to differentiate between simply having a favorable feeling toward something.

correlated with the number of audience impressions and clicks. Emotions could, in turn, affect attitudes: A report on an experimental study focused on extremist propaganda (Braddock, 2019) says that attitudes toward an extremist group—and intent to support the group—were found to be at least partly driven by emotional reactions to information, particularly anger.

CHAPTER THREE

How the Experiment Was Conducted

To study the effect of various propaganda interventions, we used a randomized controlled trial with a control group and three treatment conditions. We recruited participants from Facebook and asked them to view and respond to several types of social media content, with treatment consisting of different interventions.

Participant Recruitment

Study participants were recruited using targeted Facebook ads (Figure 3.1). These ads targeted users 18 years of age and older who resided in California, Nevada, and Arizona.[1] The ads offered participants a chance to earn up to $30 by participating in three waves of surveys. By the end of the recruitment phase, the Facebook ads had reached 762,624 unique profiles and generated 6,968 clicks.

[1] This study was sponsored by an agency of the government of the State of California; therefore, we wanted to primarily recruit participants from that state. We recognized, however, that California residents lean left on the political spectrum, with 46 percent registered as Democrats and 24 percent as Republicans (Public Policy Institute of California, 2020b). It was important, given the political nature of Russian propaganda, that our sample represent both right- and left-leaning political audiences. Consequently, we also recruited participants from Arizona and Nevada. Residents in Arizona are evenly balanced between those registered to vote Democratic versus Republican: 34.8 percent and 32.4 percent, respectively (Secretary of State, State of Arizona, undated). Nevada residents lean left by only a five-point margin: 38.2 percent for Democrats to 33.2 percent for Republicans (Office of Nevada Secretary of State, 2020).

Figure 3.1
Facebook Advertisement for Participant Recruitment

Clicking on the Facebook ad took users to our baseline survey, hosted on a separate website. Participants consented to participate, were screened for study eligibility based on age and state of residence, and affirmed their willingness to "commit to thoughtfully provide your best answers to this survey." Participants immediately completed the baseline survey that asked about demographic information, internet and social media use, news consumption habits, political views, and other metrics described later in this chapter. The baseline survey also collected email addresses for use in administering subsequent surveys and distributing the incentive payments.

After the baseline survey was completed, we used a stratified randomization strategy to assign participants to one of four treatment conditions using age (younger or older than 40 years), state of residence, gender, and self-reported political ideology (lean left, lean right, or neither). One week after completing the baseline survey, participants received an email with a link for the Survey Test Session and were paid $15 in Amazon credits for their time.[2] A total of 1,796 participants completed the baseline survey (out of a total of 2,261 who attempted to enroll).[3] Of these, 1,529 completed the follow-up survey. This study was approved by RAND's Human Subjects Protection Committee.

Three Groups Received Interventions

The overall study design is depicted in Figure 3.2. One week after participants completed their baseline survey, they were exposed to a set of pretest content and a set of carefully cultivated memes that we refer to as the *disinformation test tranche.* This test tranche contained 12 memes drawn from previous Russian propaganda campaigns, false news, real news, and public service announcements (PSAs). Participants were first shown the pretest content and then immediately exposed to the disinformation test tranche.

The treatment conditions of this study are defined by variations in either the pretest content or the disinformation test tranche. The pretest content contained either media literacy content (video or memes) or a set of placebo memes containing no lesson on media literacy. The disinformation test tranche contained a set of memes that either made references to the source of those memes or contained no reference to the source. The four treatment conditions can be summarized as follows:

- **Control Group (blind to source):** In the pretest, participants viewed six placebo memes that contained no media literacy content (see Figure A.1).[4] The memes used in the disinformation test tranche contained no reference to the source.

---

2 Note that participants were also asked to complete a second survey test session approximately one week after they completed the first survey test session. Participants received another $15 in Amazon credits for completing this second session. The data from this session are not presented in this report.

3 Among those attempting to enroll, 158 potential participants were ineligible, one refused the consent, 131 were deemed duplicates, and 175 did not complete the entire survey.

4 Included in the pretest content were two inspirational memes, two advertisement memes, and two PSA memes.

Figure 3.2
Study Design

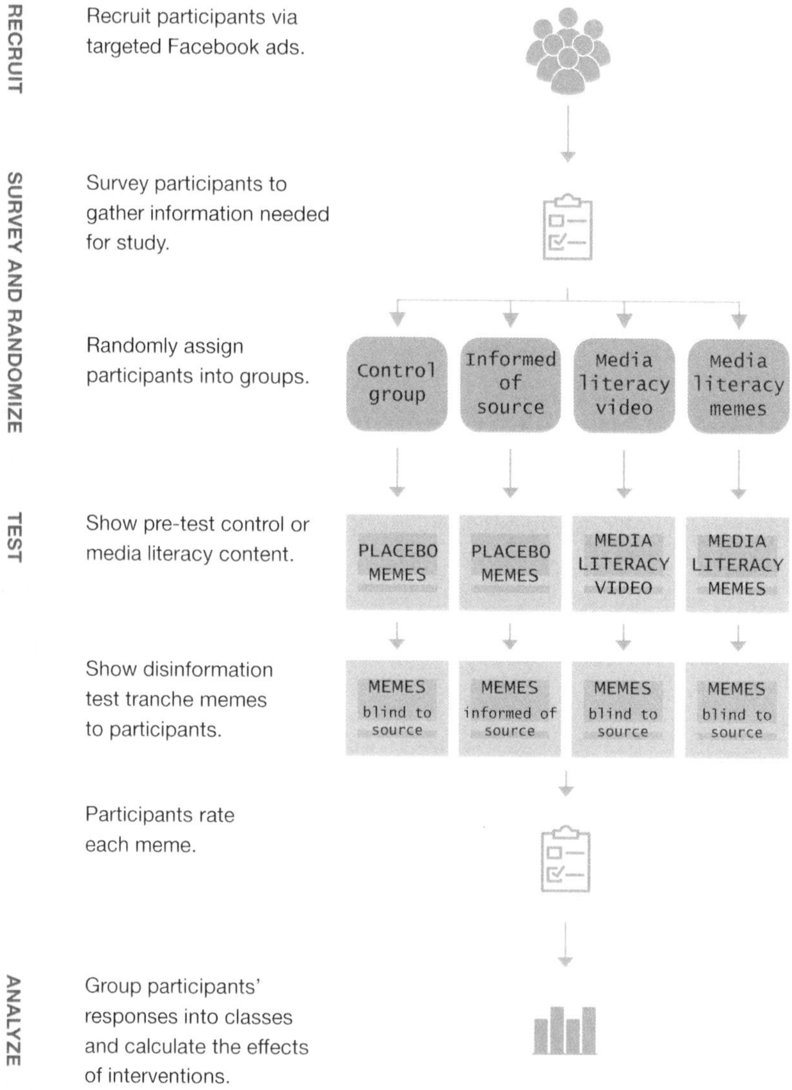

- **Source Provided:** In the pretest, participants also viewed six placebo memes that contained no media literacy content. The memes used in the disinformation test tranche contained a statement that made explicit reference to the source of those memes. In the case of all the Russian propaganda memes, for example, that statement read, "Source: The Russian government, which recently disseminated this and other social media memes as part of a covert propaganda campaign in the United States."
- **Media-Literacy Video:** In the pretest, participants were shown a 97-second video on media literacy. In the video, a narrator explains how social media platforms feed users new content that is similar to material that they have interacted with before; the narrator also describes ways to avoid becoming trapped in this bubble of like-minded content, to seek alternative points of view, and to evaluate sources.[5] The memes used in the disinformation test tranche contained no reference to the source.
- **Media-Literacy Memes:** In the pretest, participants were shown six memes, two of which contained an explicit lesson on media literacy (see Figure A.2).[6] The memes used in the disinformation test tranche contained no reference to the source.

---

[5] The media-literacy video was provided to RAND by IREX, a global development and education organization (IREX, undated). IREX has developed media-literacy educational curricula, and it implements media-literacy training programs globally. IREX's educational programs have supplemented their training with PSAs that offer condensed and brief lessons on media literacy. Given the coronavirus disease 2019 (COVID-19) pandemic, it was not possible to create a new tailored video to address the nuanced characteristics of Russian propaganda. Instead, IREX drew from a preexisting animated video that was 1 minute and 37 seconds in length and was part of a longer online course called "Very Verified" that blended short videos with in-person discussion.

[6] IREX also provided RAND with media-literacy memes. These were adopted from a "Wash Your News" social media campaign on media literacy that used memes to convey six lessons for responsible social media use (see Figure A.2). These messages represent key pillars of IREX's media literacy approach, and are usually taught as part of interactive, skill-building training initiatives. Each participant in the media literacy memes group was shown a set of two randomly selected memes. The key themes of the six memes are as follows:

- **Take back your brain:** A "name it to tame it" meme warns audiences that highly emotional narratives or images are often an attempt at manipulation. It urges audiences to name the emotion they are feeling and consider what the creator is trying to accomplish.

A Mix of Russian Propaganda, False News Headlines, and Factual Content

The disinformation test tranche contained a mix of Russian propaganda, false news headlines, real news headlines, and public service announcements. The vast majority of Russian propaganda memes used in this study were selected from a compilation of social media advertisements (U.S. House of Representatives Permanent Select Committee on Intelligence, 2015–2017). A small subsample of memes was drawn from a 2019 report by the technology research and design firm, Graphika (François, Nimmo, and Eib, 2019). (The Russian memes used in this study are depicted in Figures A.3 to A.5 with underlying notes identifying the source of the memes.)

The 12 items in the test tranche were drawn from the following six specific categories. Table 3.1 provides additional information on the content of these memes and the selection criteria.

- **Right-leaning Russian memes:** Each participant viewed two Russian memes (randomly drawn from a total pool of 11) targeting right-leaning audiences (Figure A.3). Each meme promoted one of four beliefs or group identities:
  - *Anti-immigration* memes conveyed a negative image of refugees or immigrants with suggestions that immigrants are illegally voting, taking benefits from veterans or breaking into people's homes.

- **Consult multiple sources:** A "verify then trust" meme urges audiences to verify the source of social media content.
- **Ditch your digital addiction:** A "turn off autopilot" meme urges audiences to take a break from addictive social media and applications and to resist clickbait.
- **Get outside your information bubble:** This meme urges audiences to "diversify your information space to include credible, well-researched sources and evidence-based guidance."
- **Take 20 seconds to reflect on what you see before you share it:** This meme warns audiences about misinformation and urges them to take 20 seconds to "reflect on what you see" before sharing it online.
- **Be mindful of your information space:** The meme urges audiences to "take stock of how much social media you consume and set boundaries to avoid being influenced and overwhelmed."

Table 3.1
Selection of Memes for the Disinformation Test Tranche

Source	Meme Category	Meme Selection	Rationale for Meme Selection
Russian propaganda	Right-leaning	Each participant viewed two randomly selected memes, one from a set of anti-immigrant or pro-Southern Confederacy–themed memes and one from a set of gun rights or religion-focused memes.	We sought to avoid memes that directly referenced the political campaigns of former Vice President Joseph Biden or President Donald Trump.
	Left-leaning	Each participant viewed two randomly selected memes, one from a set of Bernie Sanders or Black-rights–themed memes and one related to gender and sexual minority rights or generic liberal issues.	Russian left-leaning memes appear less issue-specific and more focused on cultural identity; our selections represent this focus.
	Pro-U.S.	Each participant viewed two randomly-selected memes, one pro-veteran meme and one patriotic pro-U.S. meme.	We selected these memes in part because they appeared less partisan and might appeal to a large cross-section of our sample.
News	False news	Each participant viewed one meme randomly selected from a group of COVID-19 related false news stories and one from a selection of generic false news stories.	We sought to avoid partisan false news stories. Memes related to COVID-19 reflected prevailing conspiracies circulating on that topic. Identifying nonpartisan generic false news memes was more difficult and we selected content from a website that some might consider satirist in nature.
	Real news	Each participant viewed one meme randomly selected from a group of real news stories related to COVID-19 and one from a selection of generic real news stories.	In seeking nonpartisan sources, we selected PBS.com and APNews, which a recent Gallup survey identified as the most unbiased providers of news. We also selected stories that we considered interesting and shareable.
PSAs	PSAs	Each participant viewed two randomly selected PSA memes selected from DigitalSynopsis.com ("60 Powerful Issue Ads . . .," undated).	We sought nonpartisan content that carried a "point of view" and appeared interesting and shareable.

- *Pro-Confederacy* memes used the imagery of the Confederate flag in messages that promote Southern heritage (or, in one case, gun rights).
- *Gun-rights* memes all promoted the Second Amendment and focused on the right of American citizens to keep and bear arms.
- *Devout Christian* memes referenced imagery of Jesus Christ in two cases; a third merged references to prayer and gun rights.

• **Left-leaning Russian memes:** Each participant viewed two Russian memes (randomly drawn from a total pool of 12) targeting left-leaning audiences (Figure A.4). Each meme was thematically associated with one of four groups:
  - *Black rights* memes promoted themes of Black pride, police brutality, and in one case, urged Blacks not to vote.
  - *Sexual and gender minority* memes all focused on pride of the lesbian, gay, bisexual, and transsexual community.
  - *Generic liberal* memes conveyed a very generic "born liberal" message, contrasted liberal and conservative positions on health care or contrasted South Carolina spending on education versus incarceration.
  - *Bernie Sanders* memes all promoted Bernie Sanders for the Democratic nomination to the presidential election.

• **Pro-U.S. Russian memes**: Each participant viewed two Russian memes (randomly drawn from a total pool of eight) showcasing U.S. pride (Figure A.5). Each meme was thematically associated with one of two groups:
  - *Pro-veteran* memes used various imagery, including flags and images of soldiers conveying pride in U.S. veterans.
  - *Pro-U.S.* memes were drawn from the Russian "Being Patriotic" Facebook page. They used imagery of U.S. veterans, the Apollo Moon landing, and a text image to convey a message of pride in the United States.

• **False headlines:** Each participant viewed two memes (randomly drawn from a total pool of ten) exemplifying false news content. One meme represented false news content related to COVID-19;

the other represented generic false news content. Only nonpartisan false news headlines were selected (Figures A.6 and A.7).

- *COVID-19 related false news* memes conveyed messages related to pandemic-related sales of AR-15 assault weapons, high HIV related death rates caused by COVID-19 service disruptions, the safety of coronavirus-related vaccine research and vaccination campaign, and a message that suggests that Belgian company AB InBev, the parent company of Corona Beer, is suing the government of China.
- *Generic false news* memes included messages that asserted that a hairdresser was arrested for making voodoo dolls from customer's hair, a 16-year-old was arrested for breaking into a hair salon and giving himself a haircut, a Japanese whaling crew was eaten alive by killer whales, a lottery winner was arrested for dumping manure on the lawn of his ex-boss, and courts allowed a New Jersey brother and sister to marry.

• **True headlines:** Each participant viewed two memes exemplifying genuine news content, drawn from ten nonpartisan AP news headlines. One meme presented content related to COVID-19; the other presented more-generic news content (Figures A.8 and A.9).

- *Authentic COVID-19-related* memes presented stories related to high rates of COVID-19 in federal prison populations, the ramping up of the federal vaccine research, a priest's use of a squirt gun to remind parishioners to maintain physical distance, the use of mannequins in a famous restaurant to help promote physical distancing, and the use of small and free libraries to offer solace during the pandemic.
- *Authentic generic news* memes highlighted such stories as the European Space Agency announcing that human urine could help make concrete on the moon, an NFL player accused of armed robbery, the announcement by CBS of a "third *Star Trek*" series, a historical anthropology article on the origins of humans in Europe, and a story on the Tibetan demand that China disclose the fate of a boy taken away in 1995.

• **PSAs:** Each participant viewed two nonpartisan memes randomly drawn from a total pool of ten (Figure A.10).

- *PSA* memes addressed topics related to school bus safety, autism, global warming, neglected children, breast cancer, first aid training, the building of handicapped-accessible facilities, animal cruelty, exploitation of workers, and treatment for schizophrenia.

Whether and How Participants Engage with the Content

The outcomes of interest measure participants' attitudes and self-reported or hypothetical behaviors toward the content. These measures are shown in Table 3.2. For all pretest content and test tranche content, participants were asked whether they would "like" or share the content if they saw it on social media and to rate how much they liked or disliked the content on a 5-point scale. For test tranche content, participants were also asked to choose how the content made them feel, selecting all that apply from a list of nine emotions.

Participants' Political Beliefs, Susceptibility to Falsehoods, and News Sources

The baseline survey collected additional information about participants that both theory and prior research implied might have a bearing on the effects of Russian propaganda. These characteristics are both behavioral and attitudinal, and they affect both the types of content that a person might see and how they might react.

To measure online behavior, we asked participants which social media platforms they use, the amount of time they spend on social media each day, and how frequently they engage with content by "liking" or sharing others' posts and posting their own content. We also asked how participants got most of their news (e.g., social media, print newspapers, television news) and which of 29 different news sources they read in any form.[7]

---

[7] The news sources we listed were the following: ABC (American Broadcasting Company) News, BBC, Breitbart, Business Insider, BuzzFeed, CBS News, CNN, Daily Caller, Fox News, *The Guardian*, *The Hill*, HuffPost, MSNBC, NBC (National Broadcasting Company) News, *New York Times*, *Newsweek*, NPR (National Public Radio), One America News Network (OANN), PBS (Public Broadcasting Service), *Politico*, Rush Limbaugh Show, Sean Hannity Show, *Time*, Univision, *USA Today*, Vice, Vox, *Wall Street Journal*, and *Washington Post*.

Table 3.2
Meme and Video Rating Scale

Question Text [answer format]	Answer Options	Content Category
How does this meme make you feel? [select all that apply]	• Happy • Excited • Sad • Angry • Scared • Hopeful • Confused • Fine • Disappointed	Test tranche only
If you saw this meme on Facebook, how likely would you be to do the following: a. Click the "like" button? b. Share with your Facebook friends?	Scale of 1 (extremely unlikely) through 5 (extremely likely)	Pretest content and test tranche
How much do you like or dislike this meme?	Scale of 1 (dislike very much) through 5 (like very much)	Pretest content and test tranche

NOTE: For the video rating scale, references to "meme" were replaced with "video." Participants in the media literacy video group also were asked to provide a free response answer to the questions "What did you like most about this video?" and "What did you like least about this video?"

Because propaganda is targeted to extremes, individuals might react differently to it depending on what the literature calls *congenial* content (Box 3.1). We collected multiple measures of participants' political beliefs. First, we asked a variation of the commonly used National Election Studies (NES) measure of political party affiliation, in which participants first report whether they tend to identify more strongly with the Democratic or Republican party. Those who reported "neither" were prompted to describe their political affiliation as they chose. The NES measure is an imperfect gauge of people's political beliefs, so we also asked participants about their views of each party.[8]

Several additional questions measured various aspects of participants' cognition using measures that prior studies have demonstrated are correlated with susceptibility to false news and conspiracy theories.

---

[8] For a discussion of shortcomings in the NES, see Greene, 2002, which recommends alternative measures that address affect or attitudes toward political parties.

Box 3.1

Targeting the Extremes

Because Russian propaganda is targeted to extreme ends of the political spectrum, individuals might react differently to different pieces of content depending on whether it is in keeping with their beliefs.

First, participants were asked whether they agree with the statement, "If I pay attention to different sources of news, I can avoid being misinformed." (Possible responses were on a 5-point scale: "strongly agree," "somewhat agree," "neither agree nor disagree," "somewhat disagree," or "strongly disagree.") Prior research (Maksl, Ashley, and Craft, 2015) has found that those who agree with a similar battery of questions have higher levels of media literacy. Participants were also asked whether they agree with the statement, "Coronavirus was purposely created and released by powerful people as part of a conspiracy." Belief in conspiracy theories—even theories that are not overtly political—is correlated with extreme political views by virtue of cognitive processes that privilege certain types of information over others (van Prooijen, Krouwel, and Pollet, 2015). Finally, we also administered the cognitive reflection test (CRT) created by Frederick, 2005. Each of three mathematical questions has a seemingly obvious "intuitive" but wrong answer and a less obvious correct answer that requires a bit more thinking.[9] CRT scores (on a scale of 0 to 3) measure the tendency to engage in analytic thinking beyond first impressions. Following studies in the psychology literature, we describe people with lower CRT scores as more intuitive and with

[9] For the CRT, participants are specifically asked, "Below are several problems that vary in difficulty. Try to answer as many as you can." The three questions included

- "A bat and a ball cost $1.10 in total. The bat costs $1.00 more than the ball. How much does the ball cost?" (Correct answer: 5 cents)
- "If it takes 5 machines 5 minutes to make 5 widgets, how long would it take 100 machines to make 100 widgets?" (Correct answer: 5 minutes)
- "In a lake, there is a patch of lily pads. Every day, the patch doubles in size. If it takes 48 days for the patch to cover the entire lake, how long would it take for the patch to cover half of the lake?" (Correct answer: 47 days)

higher CRT scores as more analytical.[10] Prior research (Pennycook and Rand, 2019) shows that more-analytical people are less susceptible to effects of certain types of disinformation.

Types of News Consumption and Emotional Responses to Content

Our analysis comprised two stages. In the first stage, we classified participants' news consumption and emotional responses using exploratory latent class analysis (LCA).[11] This reduced the number of dimensions and grouped the responses into conceptually coherent classes or "types" that could be compared and used in analysis. In the second stage, we examined control group patterns to establish a connection between emotions and behaviors; we then calculated treatment effects.

We used LCA in two ways for this analysis. As we will detail in Chapter Five, we used LCA to bin participants into different categories that varied according to which of the 29 different news sources they had read in the past week.

LCA was also used to categorize emotional responses to the content. Participants were asked to list which of nine possible emotions were elicited by each piece of social media content. Because a participant might have a different emotional response to each meme, we conducted a separate LCA for each of the six test tranche categories (right-leaning Russian meme, left-leaning Russian meme, etc.). The unit of observation was a *person-meme*—i.e., one observation for each meme each person viewed. The result is a different "type" of emotional response for each meme.

In addition, because responses might differ depending on treatment condition, we fit the LCA model to the control group only. These response patterns correspond to emotional reactions to seeing each meme without any source information or media literacy intervention—the closest approximation we have to participants' natural reactions to seeing memes on their Facebook timelines. We then used the LCA model to do an out-of-sample classification of response patterns from other treatment

---

[10] Pennycook and Rand, 2020, use the terms "intuitive" and "deliberative."

[11] LCA is a statistical method for identifying class membership among participants without imposing additional assumptions about the number of classes or their composition.

conditions. The classifications, therefore, tell us whether the distribution of emotional responses changes under different treatment conditions, as benchmarked by the response patterns observed with no treatment intervention. We use these resulting emotional response classes as outcome variables to calculate treatment effects in our survey.

Sample Characteristics and Classification of Emotional Responses

Sample Characteristics

We used the 1,529 follow-up participants for analysis. Average characteristics are listed in Figure 3.3 and grouped thematically. (The 29 news sources are not listed separately; see Figure B.1 for average readership in this sample.)

This project was funded by the State of California, so we first considered whether the participants were representative of that state. Because our sample is drawn from the population of Facebook users and encompasses people from outside California, we would not expect it to be representative of California overall. Nevertheless, a comparison is instructive for understanding external validity of the study. Our sample has more women than men and, compared with California as a whole, a lower proportion is Hispanic but a larger proportion is Black or Non-Hispanic White. The sample also underrepresents foreign-born individuals. The median age of the sample is roughly the same as of Californians overall (36 years old).[12] The sample also evenly represents those whose political beliefs lean left and those who lean right, at least compared with California voter registration statistics.[13]

---

[12] The comparison statistics come from the Public Policy Institute of California, 2020a. These say that, as of 2018, 39 percent of Californians were Latino, 37 percent were White, 6 percent were Black, and 27 percent were foreign-born; the median age was 36.7 years old.

[13] Among registered California voters, 46 percent are Democrats and 24 percent are Republicans (Public Policy Institute of California, 2020b).

Figure 3.3
Characteristics of Test Session 1 Participants

DEMOGRAPHICS

	Mean (%)
California	80
Arizona	8
Nevada	12
Male	41
Female	59
White non-Hispanic	65
Hispanic	9
Black	18
Asian	11
Other race	2
Born in the United States	94
Evangelical Christian	30
Non-Evangelical Protestant	25
Roman Catholic	9
Other religion	14
Atheist	10
Agnostic	13
Religion important or very important	31
Employed as of January 2020	75
Unemployed in January 2020	13
Not in labor force in January 2020	13
Technical degree or high school diploma or less	13
Associate's degree or some college	25
Four-year college degree	51
Postgraduate degree	12
Household income >$75,000	50

SOCIAL MEDIA AND NEWS

	Mean (%)
Most common source of news	
Radio	7
News website or app	20
Print news or magazine	5
Local television	9
Network television	14
Cable news television	14
Social Media	27
Friends and family	6
>3 hours per day on social media	35
"Like" content on social media at least once per day	68
Repost others' content at least once per day	50
Post own content at least once per day	46
Uses Instagram	59
Uses Twitter	76
Uses Pinterest	37
Uses TikTok	30
Uses Snapchat	34
Uses Gab	5
Uses Reddit	38
Uses Tumblr	12
Uses LinkedIn	43

POLITICAL BELIEFS OR ENGAGEMENT

	Mean (%)
Left-leaning political beliefs	46
Right-leaning political beliefs	30
Lean neither left nor right	24
Voted in 2018 midterm election	84
Registered to vote at current address	90
Follow political news "often" or "very often"	73
Favorable view of Democrats	54
Favorable view of Republicans	37
Unfavorable view of both	24

COGNITIVE AND ANALYTIC

	Mean (%)
Agree: "Reading many news sources helps me stay informed"	85
Agree: COVID-19 is a conspiracy	25
CRT score	
0	25
1	10
2	19
3	47

NOTE: Sums of various sets of variables might not add to 100 percent because of rounding. Less than 1 percent of the sample reported the following categories, which are not listed here: nonbinary gender; other social media platforms.

Emotional Responses: Positive or Negative

The LCA of emotional responses identified two types of responses for each of the six sets of test content.[14] These two types map neatly to response patterns in which participants chose primarily positive emotions (hopeful, excited, happy, or fine) or primarily negative emotions (sad, angry, confused, disappointed, or scared). We therefore classify the overall emotional response to each meme as a *positive* reaction or a *negative* one. Figure 3.4 shows the frequency with which each of the nine individual emotions was reported for responses classified as positive or negative. There is a stark divide, with very few cases in which both positive and negative emotions were chosen at the same time.

For the remainder of the analysis, we use a positive reaction as a primary outcome of interest, using probit regressions to determine whether treatment interventions changed participants' emotional reactions to different memes.

---

[14] For some sets of test content, a three-class model fit slightly better than the two-class model. In these cases, the three classes represented a "positive" response, "negative" response, and a third class in which participants reported feeling "fine" or "confused" with few other emotions. In robustness checks with three classes instead of two we found that the results were consistent when comparing the probability of a "positive" response with one of the other two types.

Figure 3.4
Frequency of Specific Emotions, by Overall Type of Emotional Response

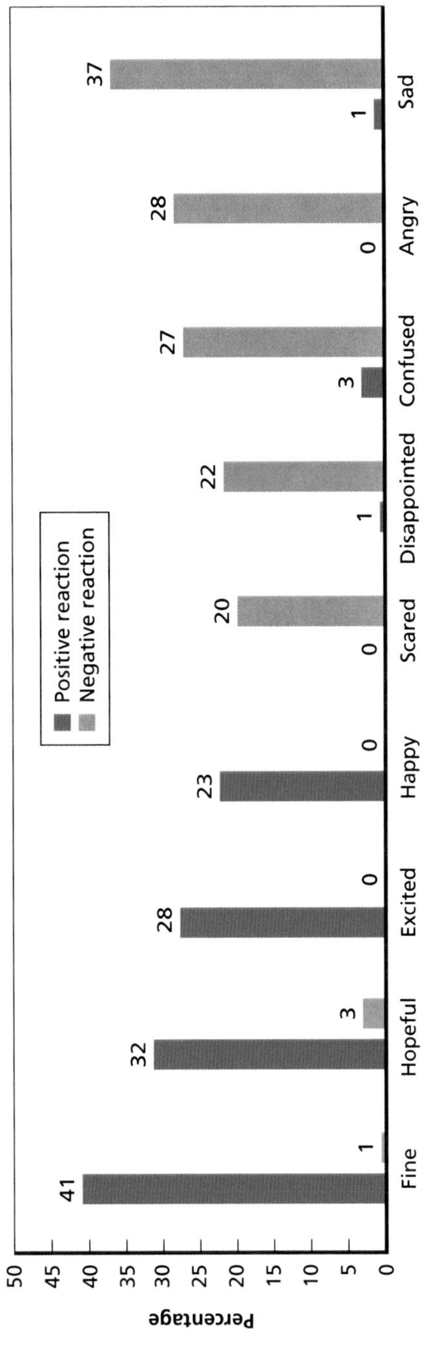

CHAPTER FOUR

Partisanship and Responses to Russian Propaganda

As noted in Chapter One, Russia has sought to influence Americans in part by disseminating highly partisan content on social media. The goal, we believe, is for this content to ultimately stoke political divisions in the United States. Analyses of past Russian theoretical work on propaganda, specifically reflexive control theory, suggests that the reactions engendered by this content might hold the key to its influence potential. In this chapter, we attempt to assess this premise, at least partially. We also assess whether we can attenuate audience reactions to that content by examining the results of our testing three potential intervention techniques.

First, we analyze how participants reacted to Russia propaganda. We show that Russian propaganda generates positive emotional reactions in politically congenial audiences and that a positive emotional response is correlated with the intention to "like" and share the content. Because of this connection, we use a *positive* response as one of our primary outcome measures.[1] We then analyze how the three treatment groups reacted to the content. We show that informing audiences of the source of Russian content blunts their emotional reaction but has limited effect on their intention to "like" or share that content.

---

[1] Braddock, 2019, establishes an association between *negative* emotions (especially anger) and decreased support for propaganda. In our analysis, the ultimate outcome of interest is not support but rather intent to engage by "liking" and sharing, which we show is correlated with a *positive* response. Thus we use "positive" as our outcome rather than "negative." By construction, however, a decrease in positive responses implies an increase in negative responses, so our results do not necessarily contradict prior work.

Control Group Showed a Partisan Divide in Reactions

In this section, we analyze the relationship between the political attitudes of participants and their reactions to Russian propaganda memes. We show that Russian content is particularly effective at generating positive emotional responses along partisan lines. The partisan divide in emotional responses is stronger for Russian content than for news items, PSAs, or even false news. Furthermore, emotional responses appear to drive behavior: A positive reaction increases the likelihood that a person will interact with content, and the stronger the reaction, the larger the effect. These findings are in line with our predictions of how Russian propaganda works.

To conduct this analysis, we analyzed results from our control group (participants were shown the memes in the disinformation test tranche without any media literacy intervention and without any source information provided). To examine emotional reactions, we used a variable indicating "positive" response to a particular meme. To compare behavioral outcomes, we constructed two variables indicating the participant was "extremely likely" or "somewhat likely" to "like" the content or to share or repost the content on social media.

Figure 4.1 shows how these three outcome measures vary by type of content and political belief. First, panel (a) illustrates how participants are more likely to have a positive response when shown memes that are politically congruent—that is, in line with their political leanings. Among left-leaning participants, 56 percent of responses to politically left-leaning Russian content were positive compared with 31 percent for politically right-leaning content.[2] Conversely, among politically right-leaning participants, 48 percent of reactions to right-leaning content were positive compared with 38 percent of responses to left-leaning content. Moreover, pro-U.S. Russian propaganda received a uniformly high rate of positive responses—more than any other set of test content. Across all political beliefs, responses to pro-U.S. content were positive at least 57 percent of the time.[3]

---

[2] It is unclear why left-leaning participants responded this positively to right-leaning content.

[3] In contrast, there is no variation in response to PSAs and little variation in response to false headlines. Right-leaning participants were somewhat more likely to have a positive response to real news memes.

Figure 4.1
Baseline Responses by Test Tranche Group and Political Partisanship

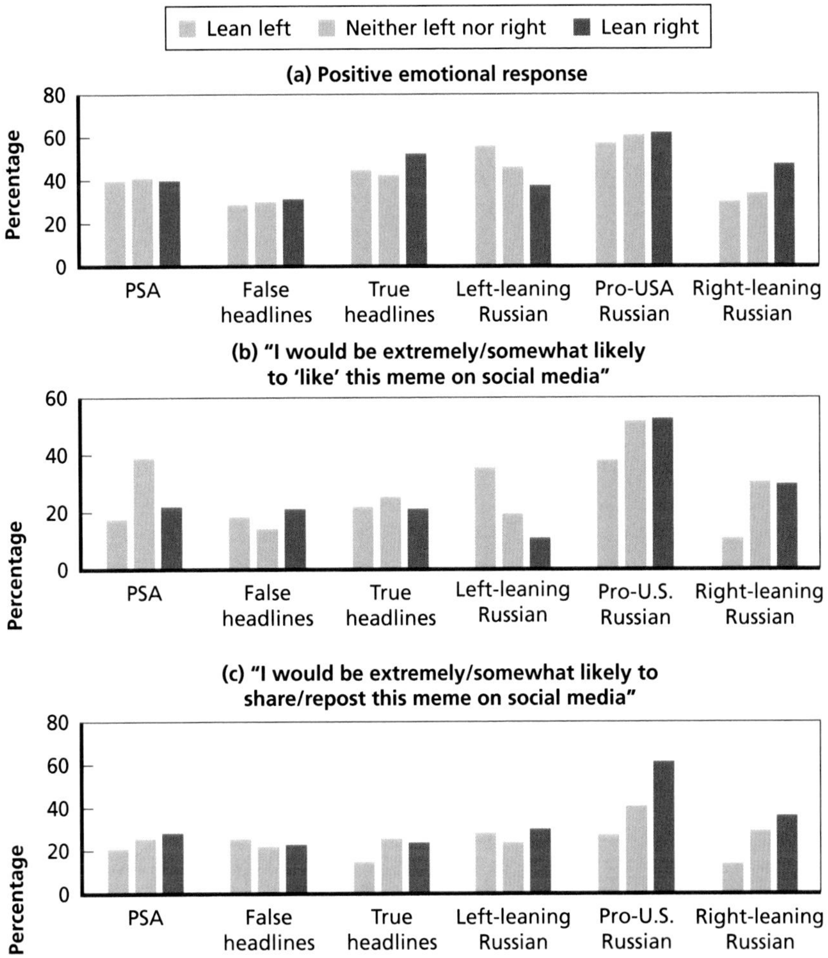

NOTES: In panel (a), participants have a stronger positive emotional response to Russian content that is congruent with their political opinions. In panels (b) and (c), because social media habits differed by political beliefs, these panels show regression-adjusted means after controlling for daily social media activity and the types of social media platforms that participants use.

Panels (b) and (c) show results for the self-reported likelihood of "liking" or sharing memes if participants were to see them in their news feeds.[4] Again, partisan differences are stronger for Russian-produced content than for other content. Participants are substantially more willing to "like" politically congruent memes and less likely to "like" memes aimed at the other side of the political divide. Right-leaning participants are more likely to say they will share politically congruent Russian content and Russian pro-U.S. memes.

User Interaction More Likely for Material That Generates Strong Positive Reactions

We suggest in the introduction that political memes, such as those used by Russia, can generate an emotional response in participants and that prior research suggests that such emotional responses are key to audience engagement with that content. To assess whether that pattern held up for this data set, we performed a regression analysis on the control group to determine whether emotional responses predicted a participant's willingness to interact with content (self-reported "likes" and shares). For this analysis, we measured the magnitude of participants' sentiment in addition to the direction (positive or negative). We used the 5-point Likert scale (from 1 [Dislike very much] through 5 [Like very much]) indicating the participant's sentiment toward each meme. We constructed a variable denoting a "strong" response, which indicates that the participant said they either liked or disliked the content "very much" as opposed to "somewhat" or "neither like nor dislike."[5]

---

[4] Because social media habits differed by political beliefs, panels (b) and (c) show regression-adjusted means after controlling for daily social media activity and the types of social media platforms that participants use.

[5] The reported sentiment and the latent emotional classes do not have a perfect correspondence. For 21 percent of the times that participants reported disliking the content, they checked off mostly positive emotions. Conversely, 44 percent of the time that participants reported liking the content, they checked off mostly negative emotions. The difference in these percentages could be indicative of social desirability bias, meaning that some participants said they liked the content despite having a negative reaction. It could also be that participants liked or disliked something concrete about a meme (such as the image) but had a different emotional response to the message, making the two responses not congruent. To

Table 4.1 shows the results. As predicted, participants are more willing to "like" and share if they have a strong reaction or a positive reaction, although the association is greater for positive reactions than for negative ones. Specifically, a strong negative reaction *reduces* intention to "like" and share by about 4 percentage points, but a strong positive reaction increases intentions to "like" and share by 25 to 29 percentage points. Participants reported that they would "like" a meme only 42 percent of the time overall, so a 29 percentage point increase is substantial.

How Did the Three Treatment Groups React to the Content?

We next analyzed the effects of our three treatments on the probability of a participant having a positive emotional response and the probability of that person "liking" or sharing the memes of the disinformation test tranche. We calculated the treatment effects using the following probit regression specification:

$$Y_{in} = \alpha + \beta_2 (Source)_i + \beta_3 (LiteracyVideo)_i + \beta_4 (LiteracyMemes)_i + \varepsilon_{in}$$

(Eq. 1)

The outcome variable is participant *i*'s response to meme number *n*: either emotional response or their reported willingness to "like" the content. The dummy variable "Source" indicates that the participant was assigned to the treatment group that was shown the source of each meme but did not view any media literacy content. The dummy variable "LiteracyVideo" indicates the participant was assigned to the group that viewed the video on media literacy during the pretest session, and the dummy variable "LiteracyMemes" indicates the participant was assigned to the group that viewed the memes on media literacy as part of the pretest content.

address these discrepancies, we performed robustness checks with alternative specifications and found results consistent with the story we present.

Table 4.1
Effects of Emotional Responses on Willingness to "Like" or Share

Reaction	"Like"			Share		
Strong	0.092***			0.076***		
	(0.015)			(0.015)		
Positive		0.147***			0.091***	
		(0.014)			(0.014)	
Strongly negative			−0.044**			−0.043**
			(0.018)			(0.018)
Strongly positive			0.289***			0.245***
			(0.021)			(0.021)
N	4,775	4,775	4,775	4,772	4,772	4,772
Pseudo-R^2	0.065	0.075	0.091	0.066	0.068	0.087
Chi-squared	403.46	477.87	558.73	411.05	429.15	528.14

NOTE: Table shows marginal effects from probit regressions, including meme fixed effects and controls for participants' usage of social media and primary sources of news.

For each probit regression, we then calculated marginal effects of the coefficients, which give the percentage point differences in outcome for each experimental group relative to the control. Therefore, the figures in this chapter describe the interpretation in percentage points: For example, a treatment effect of –2 percent indicates that the outcome was 2 percentage points less likely for the given experimental group than for the control group.

We calculated a separate regression for each meme category (left-leaning Russian, right-leaning Russian, and so forth) to allow for different effects depending on the message theme. We also conducted subgroup analyses to examine the effects of different sets of memes on different target audiences. Appendix B provides more details on the treatment effect calculations.[6]

We present our results for emotional reactions and for willingness to "like" material, but we do not present results for willingness to share memes because there was no significant effect on sharing for the experiment as a whole.[7]

To summarize, revealing the source appears to significantly reduce the positive emotional response that participants experience when viewing either pro-U.S. Russian content or Russian content that is congruent with a participant's political views. Revealing the source also reduced the likelihood that participants would "like" the pro-U.S. memes. However, this intervention did not affect the probability that participants would "like" the political Russian content and it had no impact on sharing. Effects of the media literacy interventions were more muted, with the main effect being that the video reduced the probability of participants "liking" the pro-U.S. Russian content.

---

[6] Before calculating treatment effects, we also compared responses with pretest content to ensure that there were no pretest differences in groups' responses to placebo content.

[7] See the joint tests of statistical significance in Appendix B.

Figure 4.2
Treatment Effects on Probability of Positive Emotional Response for the Entire Sample

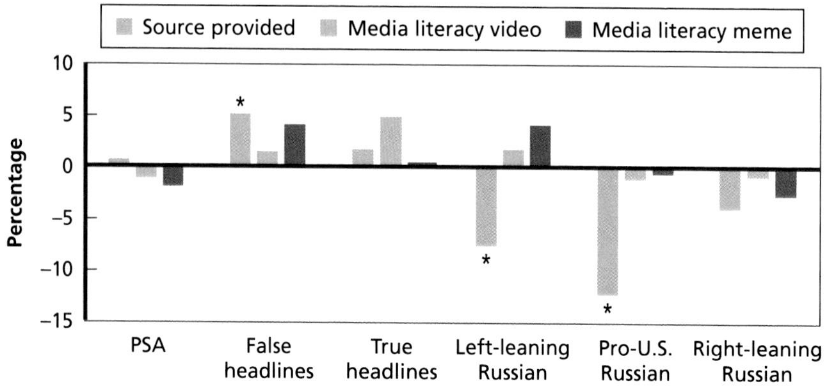

NOTE: Asterisks (*) indicate statistical significance at the 5-percent level.

Emotional Responses Most Strongly Affected by Revealing Source of Material

Figure 4.2 shows the impact of the three different treatments (revealing the source, media-literacy video, and media-literacy memes) on the probability of a positive emotional response to the presented memes.

Revealing the source had the strongest effect of all interventions, decreasing the probability of a positive response to politically left-leaning, politically right-leaning, and pro-U.S. Russian content. This effect was strongest for reactions to pro-U.S. Russian memes, with a decline of 12 percentage points in the probability that a participant would have a positive reaction to such memes. By contrast, revealing the source *increased* the proportion of positive responses to false news headlines by 5 percentage points.

The media literacy interventions had effects that were relatively moderate and not significant, apart from the video having a positive effect on participants' reactions to real news headlines.

These effects are particularly striking when we consider the political views of our participants. Figure 4.3 breaks down these effects by political partisanship for Russian and false news memes (effects for PSAs and real news were negligible and therefore not shown).

Figure 4.3
Treatment Effects on Probability of Positive Emotional Response, by Political Partisanship

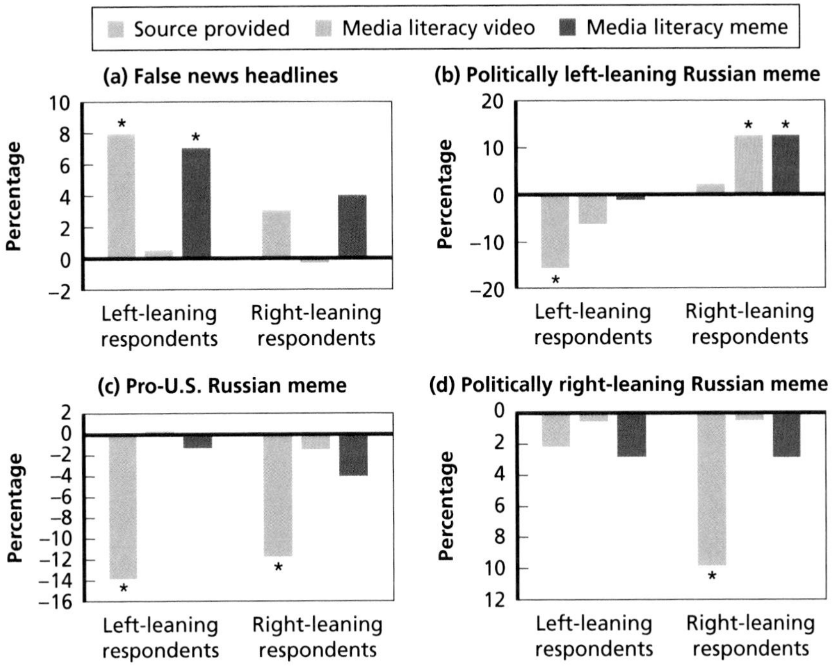

NOTE: Asterisks (*) indicate statistical significance at the 5-percent level.

Emotional responses show a clear partisan pattern: Revealing the source significantly reduces the probability of a positive response to content that is congruent with a participant's political views. It also reduces the likelihood of a positive response to pro-U.S. content for both politically left-leaning and politically right-leaning participants.

When the source is revealed, politically left-leaning participants were 15 percentage points less likely to respond positively to left-leaning disinformation, and 14 percentage points less likely to respond positively to pro-U.S. disinformation (reflecting a roughly 25-percent drop relative to our baseline). Similarly, politically right-leaning participants were 10 and 12 percentage points less likely to respond positively to right-leaning and pro-U.S. propaganda (a roughly 20-percent drop relative to our baseline). The intervention had no effect on how participants responded to viewing content that was incongruous with their political views.

Revealing the source also appears to increase the probability that politically left-leaning participants will have a positive reaction to false news headlines (8 percentage points), but it appears to have no effect on politically right-leaning participants.

In contrast, the media literacy interventions appeared to have no measurable effect on politically left-leaning participants' emotional responses to any propaganda, although the media literacy memes did increase the probability of a positive response to false news. For politically right-leaning participants, both literacy interventions significantly increased the likelihood of a positive response to left-leaning Russian content media literacy with no effect on politically congruent or pro-U.S. Russian content.

Revealing Materials' Source and Media Literacy Video Reduced "Likes" for Pro-U.S. Memes but Not Partisan Memes

Figure 4.4 shows the effects for the intent to "like" each type of disinformation test tranche meme for the entire sample. Revealing the

Figure 4.4
Treatment Effects for Intent to "Like" Content, by Type of Content

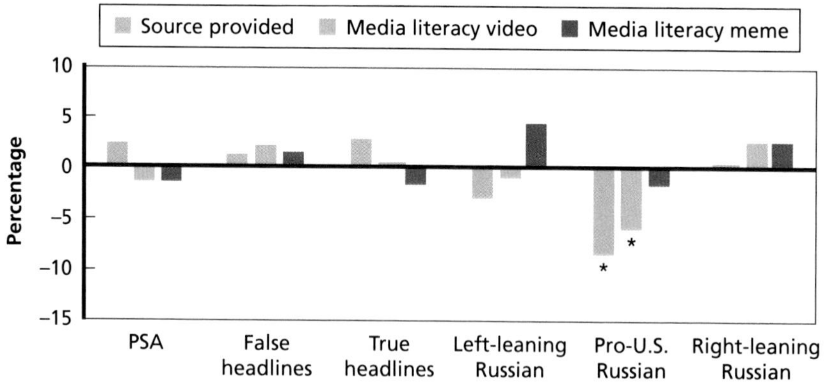

NOTE: Asterisks (*) indicate statistical significance at the 5-percent level.

source and watching the media literacy video significantly reduced the probability that participants would "like" Russian pro-U.S. content. The magnitudes of the effects are 8 and 6 percentage points, respectively, which translate to a drop of 12 to 16 percent from that probability for those who had no intervention. In contrast, all three interventions had limited impact on the probability that participants would "like" the remaining content, including the politically right-leaning and left-leaning memes.

We also analyzed the results of "liking" the content on the basis of political partisanship. The direction of the effects generally mirror those of the emotional responses, but the magnitudes are smaller and generally not statistically significant. The exception was for pro-U.S. content: Revealing the source significantly reduced politically left-leaning participants' intent to "like" such memes by 8 percentage points. The effect on politically right-leaning participants was of the same magnitude but was not significant ($p = 0.07$). We do not provide a figure illustrating these results.

CHAPTER FIVE

Politically Partisan Effects and Types of News Consumers

In this chapter, we reassess the reaction to Russian content and the three treatment arms drawing on an exploratory analysis that classifies participants according to the different sources they use to access news and information. We show that the partisan effects that underpin reactions to Russian propaganda and the impact of revealing the source are driven by two types of news consumers: the politically left-leaning *Partisan Left* and the politically right-leaning *Partisan Right* categories, which we describe in a later section of this chapter.

Specifically, we show that participants who fell into the *Partisan Left* and *Partisan Right* groups reacted in the strongest and most-partisan ways to Russian content. We also show that revealing the source generated the greatest impact on the tendency of these participants to respond positively and to "like" Russian propaganda content. Even if interventions do not change behavior across all groups and all types of content, it is promising that they might shift problematic behaviors in those most likely to engage in the first place.

The media literacy interventions also had their strongest effects among those in the *Partisan Right* and *Partisan Left* groups. We did not document positive impact on emotional responses, but we did find that exposure to the video on media literacy reduced the likelihood that those in the politically right-leaning *Partisan Right* group would "like" right-leaning and pro-U.S. content.

Creating Five Audience Categories Using News Consumption Habits

In the baseline survey, participants were asked to choose which of 29 different news sources they had read in the past week. Using LCA, we classified participants into news consumption types. Our results yielded five different types of news consumers, as detailed in Appendix B. We then assessed the personal characteristics of individuals in each class to determine what made them distinct. Personal characteristics were not part of the LCA calculations; thus, any strong association between a characteristic and news consumer type indicates that the typologies yield meaningful distinctions among news consumers.

Table 5.1 describes key characteristics that distinguish each type of news consumer, as follows:

- *Analytical Skeptics*: Members of this group were the most common type of participant, making up 40 percent of our sample. Most participants said they get their news from *USA Today*, ABC, NPR, *Time*, the *Wall Street Journal*, and BBC. This group is most evenly split in terms of the format for consuming news. Those who fall into this group are highly analytic—89 percent had perfect CRT scores—and are disenchanted with politics—46 percent reported an unfavorable view of both political parties. This group also had the most White participants (and the most Black participants) and was largely Protestant, educated, and high-earning.
- *Disengaged Intuits*: After the *Analytical Skeptics*, the next-largest number (24 percent) of participants fell into this group. The majority of these individuals report getting their news from CNN, ABC, NBC, and CBS. Accordingly, they are most likely to get their news from local, network, or cable television. They are highly intuitive (this group has the lowest average CRT score), and they read the fewest news sources (an average of three per person). Compared with the rest of the sample, these participants earned less, had less education, and were less likely to be employed.
- *Partisan Left*: The majority of the third type (13 percent of the sample) report getting news from CNN, the *New York Times*,

Table 5.1
News Consumption Types

	Analytical Skeptics (40%)	Disengaged Intuits (24%)	Partisan Left (13%)	Partisan Right (13%)	Intuitive Omnivores (10%)
Attributes					
Intuition	Highly analytical (mean CRT score: 2.8)	Highly intuitive (mean CRT: 1.0)			Highly intuitive (mean CRT: 1.3)
Political views	Most likely to dislike both political parties (46%)		Lean left (64%), most likely to view Democrats favorably (65%)	Most likely to view GOP favorably (56%)	
COVID-19			Least likely to think COVID is a conspiracy (13%)	Mostly likely to believe COVID is a conspiracy (47%)	
Social media		Least likely to use social media platforms			Spend most time on social media (51% > 3 hrs/day)
News format	Evenly split by format for obtaining news	Most likely to get news from TV (51%)	Most likely to get new from website or app (40%)	Most likely to get news from social media (50%)	Most likely to get news from website or app (40%)
News sources	Most common news source: *USA Today* (54%)	Most common news source: CNN (56%), read fewest news sources (mean: 3)	Most common news source: *New York Times* (86%)	Most common news source: Fox (39%), most likely to read far-right news outlets	Most common news source: NYTimes (87%), read largest number of news sources (mean: 14), only group besides *Partisan Right* to read far-right news outlets

Table 5.1—Continued

	Analytical Skeptics (40%)	Disengaged Intuits (24%)	Partisan Left (13%)	Partisan Right (13%)	Intuitive Omnivores (10%)
Demographics					
Race	72% white, 24% black		30% Asian		50% racial or ethnic minority
Gender			69% women	50% men	
Age	51% over age 40			76% under age 40	
College	79% with college degree	54% no college degree		60% no college degree	
Income and employment	62% earn > $75k	67% earn < $75k	28% not in labor force	62% earn < $75k	61% earn > $75k
Religion	75% Protestant or Evangelical		43% atheist or agnostic		

NPR, and the *Washington Post*. This group is most likely to get its news from a news website or app. These participants are also most likely to be politically left-leaning and to view the Democratic Party favorably, and they are least likely to believe that COVID-19 is a conspiracy. This group has the highest proportion of women, atheists or agnostics, Asians, and people not in the labor force.

- *Partisan Right*: The majority of the fourth type (13 percent), reports getting news from Fox, Buzzfeed, Sean Hannity, and *USA Today*. It is the only group for which no single news source was used by more than one-half of the participants. These participants were most likely to get news from far-right outlets: the Daily Caller, Breitbart, Rush Limbaugh, One America News Network (OANN), and others (only two of the five types get news from these outlets at all, the other group being *Intuitive Omnivores*). This type is most likely to get news via social media, most likely to believe COVID-19 is a conspiracy, and most likely to hold a favorable view of the Republican Party. Compared with other types, this group of participants was younger, had a higher proportion of men, and was less educated. Members of this group are more likely to be employed, but they have below-median incomes.
- *Intuitive Omnivores*: The least common type (10 percent), the majority of these individuals report getting their news from the *New York Times*, the *Washington Post*, NBC, CBS, and ABC (more than one-half of the participants falling into this group reported consulting each of those five outlets). These individuals get news from the greatest number of sources: 14 per person, on average. They are the only type besides those in the *Partisan Right* who get news from far-right sources. They are also highly intuitive (this group had the second-lowest average CRT score). Compared with other types, this group had the fewest White participants and more Asian and Hispanic participants, and these participants earn above-median incomes.

Our media consumption typology provides a more nuanced categorization of survey participants than does a simple division by political beliefs. It is clear that certain types do tend to lean more to the left or right politically, yet no type can be defined by political beliefs alone. Some types might be distinguished by a tendency to consult news sources that lean politically right or left, but there are spillovers among every type, with some people consulting news sources from both ends of the ideological spectrum. This observation is in line with other research showing that social media users do not inhabit pure echo chambers (Bakshy, Messing, and Adamic, 2015; Barberá, 2015). The reality is that people read more than just the content that agrees with their own views.

Other research shows that people might be more distinguished by how they interpret news than by what individual source they read (Tripodi, 2018). In line with this observation, our typology shows that certain types are distinguished by their analytical style and belief in conspiracy theories, in addition to what they read and the format in which they read it. This suggests that the typology might capture salient differences in emotional or cognitive processes that underlie the complex landscape of media consumption.

Partisan Left and *Partisan Right*: Most-Partisan Behavior Toward Russian Content

We examined whether media consumption types differed in their responses to Russian propaganda.

The results show that two groups drive the partisan effects shown in Chapter Four: *Partisan Left* and *Partisan Right*. Figure 5.1 shows the control group's reactions to Russian content and false headlines. (The figure shows the sample averages, not controlling for social media use.) Those in the *Partisan Left* and *Partisan Right* have the most-partisan reactions—as is evident in panel (a), which illustrates their different emotional reactions to politically left-leaning and right-leaning Russian content: Those more likely to react positively to politically left-leaning content are less likely to react positively to politically right-leaning content and vice-versa. The *Partisan Left* and *Partisan Right* groups are at the respective extremes.

Figure 5.1
Baseline Responses by Test Tranche Group and News Consumption Type

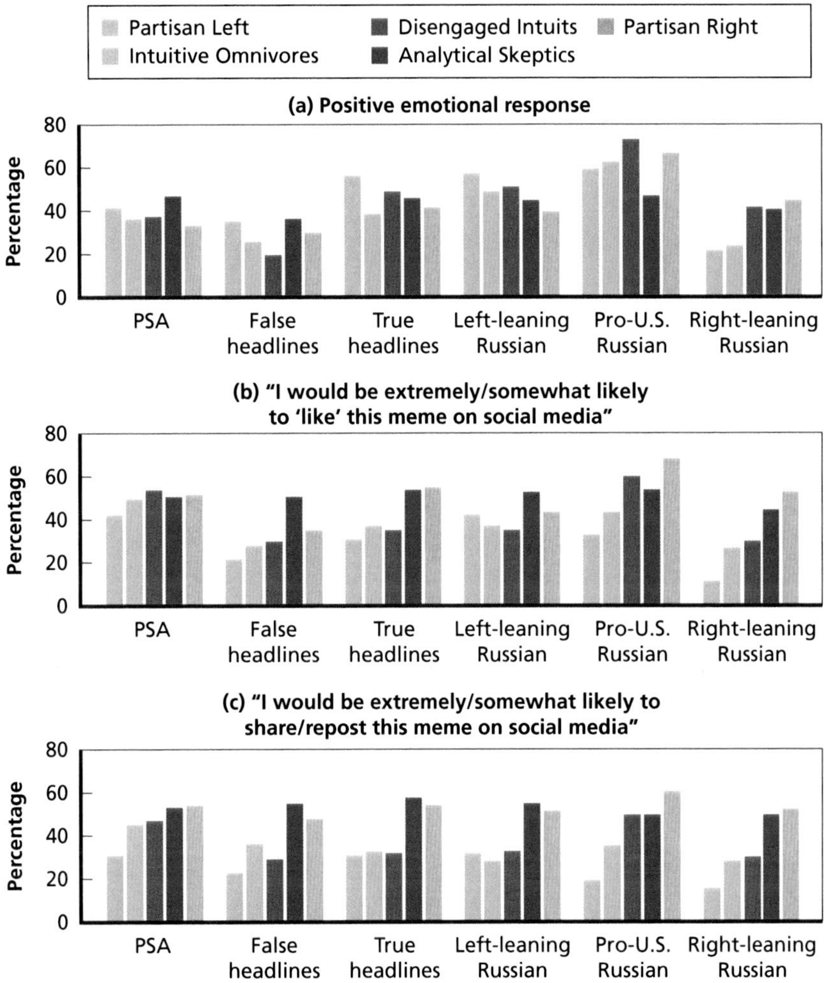

NOTE: Those in the Partisan Left react most positively to left-leaning content, most negatively to right-leaning content, and are by far the most likely to have a strong reaction to any type of content. They report greatly disliking right-leaning content and are least likely to say that they would interact with right-leaning content. Those in the Partisan Right group are at opposite extremes in terms of emotional responses and are overall most likely to interact with all types of content.

Politically right-leaning content also generates a clear partisan divide in terms of willingness to interact: Those in the *Partisan Left* are much less likely than those in the *Partisan Right* to say they would "like" or share right-leaning content—panels (b) and (c). By contrast, those in the *Partisan Right* are most likely to interact with all types of content in general, showing less of a partisan split in behavior than a general tendency to "like" and share across the board.

To summarize, the news consumer typology shows that those in the *Partisan Left* and *Partisan Right* groups react in the strongest and most-partisan ways to Russian content. Note from Figure 5.1 that these two groups are polar opposites in many ways: Those in the *Partisan Left* are most likely to lean left politically, are least likely to believe that COVID-19 is a conspiracy, and are particularly likely to read major newspapers such as the *New York Times* directly on the newspaper website or app. Those in the *Partisan Right* group are most likely to lean right politically, most likely to believe that COVID-19 is a conspiracy, most likely to consume far-right news, and most likely to get their news on social media. The partisan divide illustrated in Chapter Four is thus driven by two groups that are distinguished by more than just political ideology.

Partisan Left, Partisan Right, and Experimental Interventions

Figure 5.2 illustrates how experimental interventions changed the probability of a participant expressing a positive response to different sets of content, using the regression specification in Equation 1. Revealing the source shows the most-consistent effects for those in the *Partisan Left*, who showed a statistically significant decrease in positive emotional response across all types of Russian content. Those in the *Partisan Right* group were significantly less likely to react positively to pro-U.S. content (and also false news headlines).

The media literacy interventions appeared to have no effect on emotional responses for most content among most media consumption types, with a particularly negligible effect for those in the *Partisan Left*.

Figure 5.2
Treatment Effects on Probability of Positive Emotional Response, by News Consumption Type

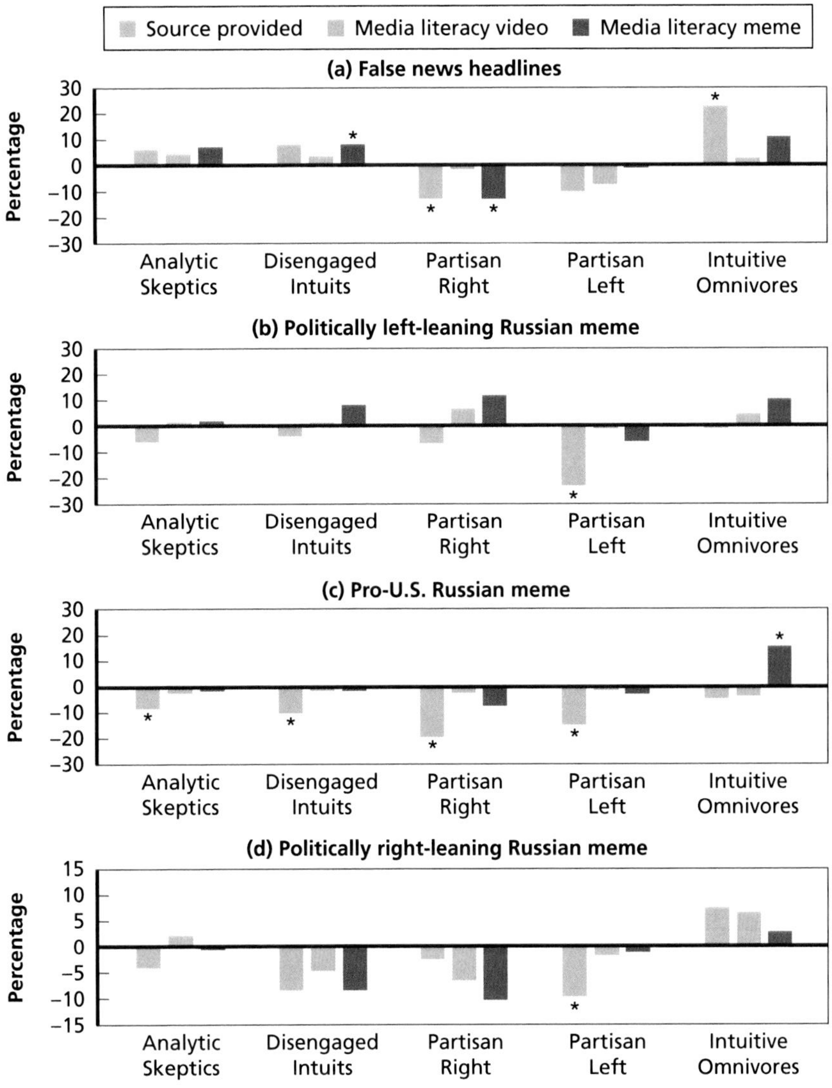

NOTE: Asterisks (*) indicate statistical significance at the 5-percent level.

Both media literacy interventions yielded moderately large effects on responses from those in the *Partisan Right* viewing right-leaning content—but these effects are not statistically significant.

The experimental effects on intent to "like" or share (not shown) again show the salience of the *Partisan Left* group in this analysis. Revealing the source significantly reduces *Partisan Left* willingness to "like" left-leaning and pro-U.S. Russian content—by about 15 percentage points (a 50-percent reduction from our baseline), with no effect on right-leaning content. Conversely, it lowers willingness among those in the *Partisan Right* group to "like" right-leaning or pro-U.S. content by a similar amount, with no effect on left-leaning content.

We also find that interventions reduced expressed willingness among those in the *Partisan Left* and *Partisan Right* groups to engage with Russian content. Figure 5.3 shows the effects on intent to "like" content for these two groups alone. We found that revealing the source significantly reduced both groups' intent to "like" pro-U.S. content and their intent to "like" content that was politically concordant with their own views, but that revealing the source had a smaller and not statistically significant effect when presented with content that was politically concordant with the other side of the political aisle. In addition, the media literacy interventions had a substantial, although not always significant, effect on those in the *Partisan Right* group, reducing their willingness to "like" politically right-leaning and pro-U.S. propaganda.[1]

Unlike the political partisanship analysis we presented in Chapter Four, the media consumption typology has identified groups with clear changes in intended behaviors toward Russian content. These behavioral effects still manifest in a partisan way, but the subpopulations driving those effects are not defined based solely on political ideology.

---

1 Note that the lack of statistical significance is partly because of small sample sizes for this analysis; effects of this size would be significant in the full sample.

Figure 5.3
Treatment Effects on Probability of "Liking" Content, by News Consumption Type

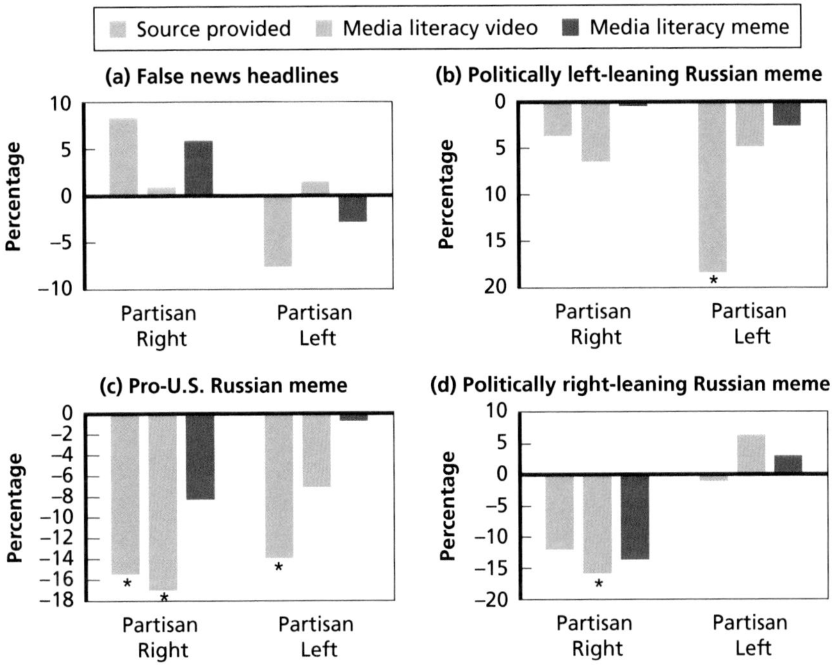

NOTE: Asterisks (*) indicate statistical significance at the 5-percent level.

CHAPTER SIX

Conclusions and Implications for Future Research

The results of our analysis show three overall patterns:

1. Russian content generates stronger emotional responses with a starker partisan divide than real news or false news content does. This emotional response appears to drive behaviors of "liking" and sharing.
2. Revealing the source of Russian content tends to reduce the probability of a positive emotional response, mostly for content that aligns with a consumer's ideology. In comparison, media literacy interventions affect emotions in different and less consistent ways—sometimes increasing the probability that a participant will react positively to Russian content but often having no effect. Neither revealing the source nor media literacy interventions appeared to affect the likelihood that partisan participants would report "liking" or sharing the partisan Russian content. However, revealing the source and the media literacy video reduce the likelihood of the entire sample sharing Russian pro-U.S. content.
3. Political partisanship effects appear driven by two different types of news consumers: those in the politically right-leaning *Partisan Right* and politically left-leaning *Partisan Left* groups. These two subgroups appear most affected by exposure to Russian propaganda that aligns with their attitudes. They also demonstrated the strongest response to the interventions. Revealing the source of Russian memes significantly reduced emotional responses among these groups to attitude-congruent content

and reduced the likelihood that they would "like" that content. Likewise, exposure to the media literacy video significantly reduced self-reported "likes" for pro-U.S. and politically right-leaning Russian propaganda among those in the *Partisan Right* group.

The major takeaway from our findings is that Russian disinformation acts effectively and strongly on individual social media users who have the strongest emotional responses, which are highly correlated with such behaviors as "liking" and sharing content. Our control group showed strong partisan divides in emotional responses to Russian content—more than for false news, real news, or PSAs. This mapped to a similar partisan divide in reported willingness to "like" or share Russian content. Participants reported greater willingness to interact with Russian memes that were politically concordant with their own views than to interact with real or false news items.

The findings that Russian content produces strong emotional reactions and that the targeted partisans are "liking" and sharing that content is problematic given the scope of the Russian propaganda campaign. Facebook estimates that at least 126 million users in the United States saw Russian-generated content between August 2015 and January 2017 (Isaac and Wakabayashi, 2017). Likewise, two congressionally funded research reports say that multiple Russian-backed social media profiles each attracted more than 100,000 followers and tens of millions of interactions, collectively generating tens of thousands of ads and hundreds of thousands of tweets (DiResta et al., 2019; Computational Propaganda Research Project, 2018).

These effects certainly appear in line with Russian interests. Our previous assessment of Russian goals and objectives, informed by an understanding of the memetic tools it employs, predict these emotional and behavioral reactions to Russian propaganda and suggest that Russia is using these reactions to spark societal division and disunity (Posard et al., 2020).

However, testing whether Russia is ultimately successful in producing these societal impacts will require further research. When exposed to attitude-congruent Russian content, do audiences harden their views on issues highlighted by that content? Does it tarnish their opinions of those who hold opposite views? And could this Russian content reach and influence such a sizable audience that it would affect the functioning of society? Research has only begun to try to answer these questions. (For example, see Bail et al., 2020).

Limitations

Our study naturally has several limitations. The ideal control group setting for the media literacy video intervention would be a condition in which participants viewed a video of similar length that does not address media literacy. Instead, our control group contained "placebo" memes; as a result, we did not control for the presentation of video content. In addition, the video on media literacy stood alone as the only pretest item presented to participants in that condition. In contrast, we presented two memes that addressed media literacy alongside four memes that did not. We did this to mimic how this content might be presented to audiences in the social media wild and to avoid unnecessarily cueing participants to the fact that this study was testing a media literacy intervention. It is possible that presentation of the lone video on media literacy might have led those participants to suspect they were in a "media literacy study" and thus react more suspiciously to the memes in the disinformation test tranche.

In addition, participants in the media literacy memes group were each randomly exposed to two out of a total of six media literacy memes. These memes offered different media literacy lessons and it is possible that some of these lessons were more successful than others in reducing self-reported "likes" or shares of Russian or false news content. Unfortunately, the sample size was not large enough to allow us to compare the relative effectiveness of the different memes.

Finally, we should note that the outcome measures assessing intended "likes" and intended shares might not fully represent the kind of activity that Facebook users demonstrate in the real world.

Setting the Right Policy and Research Agendas

Our results show that there is promise for policy interventions to mitigate Russian disinformation. Participants appear to be turned off by disinformation messaging when they learn that it was created with malign intent by a foreign organization.[1] The effect of this intervention represents an improvement of 15–25 percent over our baseline, depending on the outcome measure, and it might represent a kind of ceiling effect for what an intervention might hope to accomplish.

It is difficult to assess the degree to which revealing the source is a feasible intervention. On one hand, Facebook, Twitter, and YouTube (among other platforms) have worked to remove Russian or other state propaganda content when it is discovered. If such practices were to continue, then, theoretically, there would be limited malicious content to which a source description could be pegged. On the other hand, it is conceivable that these platforms could decide to keep such content actively available even after discovery, that other social media platforms might arise that do not have policies for removal of state-sponsored content, or that watchdog or academic institutions might be faster at uncovering state-sponsored content than the platforms. In these situations, there would be immense value in developing a third-party plug-in that can unmask the source of state-sponsored content. This would be akin to the various bot detectors that help users detect bot accounts in their Twitter feeds. (For a list of these and other online tools to fight disinformation, see RAND Corporation, undated).

Providing generalized warnings might be an alternative to directly acknowledging sources. Specifically, there might be utility in warning audiences that Russia or other state actors disseminate this type of propaganda and that audiences should be highly suspicious of sources and their intent. Clayton and her colleagues, 2019, for example, demonstrated that providing participants a general warning that subsequent content might contain false or misleading information increases the likelihood

---

[1] The fact that revealing the source blunted the emotional effects of Russian propaganda suggests that this approach might have blocked the indirect or heuristic driven pathway for propaganda influence.

that participants see false headlines as less accurate. This effect, which was deemed "relatively modest" in size, still held true when participants were confronted with attitude-congruent political content. Whether this effect extends to propagandistic content is unclear.

It also might be possible to inoculate audiences against Russian propaganda by pairing the warning with a weakened example of a Russian propaganda meme and providing directions on how to refute the meme. Studies have shown inoculation procedures to effectively induce resistance to conspiracy theories, extremist propaganda, and climate change misinformation (Cook, Lewandowsky, and Ecker, 2017; Braddock, 2019; Banas and Miller, 2013; van der Linden et al., 2017). Researchers should test inoculation's effectiveness on Russian propaganda, although the variety of topics targeted by the Russians might complicate research design.

The media literacy video might be a useful tool to counter some forms of Russian propaganda, and it might prove most successful with those in the *Partisan Right* group. Exposure to the video on media literacy significantly reduced the likelihood that participants in the entire sample would "like" Russia's pro-U.S. content and decreased the likelihood that those in the politically right-leaning *Partisan Right* group, in particular, would "like" Russian politically right-leaning and pro-U.S. memes.[2] Exposure to media literacy content did not consistently reduce the positive emotional response of participants to Russian propaganda or false news. Reducing emotional responses was never a goal of the

[2] The video on media literacy affected "likes" for propaganda but not for false news, which is often considered the usual writ for media literacy interventions. Although the reason for this is not known, it could be an artifact of design for this study. Guess, Nyhan, and Reifler, 2020, documented that a Facebook-based media literacy campaign offering ten "Tips to Spot Fake News" led to significant and persistent effects in the ability of participants to discriminate between mainstream and false news headlines (see Constine, 2017, for a description of the "Tips" campaign). Our study, in contrast, did not document an effect of media literacy content on false news. Differences in the design for both studies might explain this. First, Guess asked participants to rate the accuracy of headlines. For our study, we initially considered asking participants to rate their trust in the content, but we chose not to because of concerns that the request would be a cue that the content could be untrustworthy. In addition, the Guess study did not ask participants about hypothetical engagement with the content ("liking" or sharing). It might be that participants who accurately identify false news headlines would still be willing to share or "like" such content if it conformed to their views.

media literacy content, however; instead, the main goal was to reduce audience intentions to "like" or share Russian social media content. To this end, the media literacy content at least partially met its goal.

Both the video and the memes provided very abbreviated exposure to media literacy content. They were intended to serve as a model of low-cost and scalable media literacy education efforts and they were originally created as a complement to a broader media literacy training regimen. Most media literacy programs represent intensive educational interventions; this study offers no assessment of that type of programming. The significant effects that we documented for the video on media literacy show that even short and scalable interventions have promise in generating positive effects. We identified one audience segment, the politically right-leaning *Partisan Right*, which appears most in need of and most amenable to interventions that can reduce the impact of Russian propaganda.[3]

The LCA model used in this study was exploratory in nature, and a follow-up confirmatory analysis should be conducted to establish the validity of the identified subgroups. That said, the *Partisan Right* and *Partisan Left* subgroups might represent audiences that could uniquely benefit from interventions. The key feature of these segments is source of news, and this feature might better enable designers of interventions to identify and reach these audiences. The video on media literacy might be one such intervention. Future research might demonstrate that generalized warnings or inoculation interventions are also effective in these populations. Testing more-holistic media literacy interventions is also recommended, as is more thoroughly examining other memetic media literacy content.

A critical focus for future research is to elucidate the connections between attitudinal reactions and engagement with content. Importantly, this is a different set of causal pathways than those usually assumed for false news. Research on "fake news" has focused pri-

---

[3] All the consumption types are associated with partisan beliefs, but the correlation is not perfect. Rather, the defining characteristics of the typological categories suggest that analytic style, susceptibility to conspiracy theories, and other characteristics might influence whether Russian content has an effect and whether interventions can work.

marily on connections between exposure to a headline, belief in that headline, and further circulating the headline. In the case of Russian disinformation, the concepts of belief and agreement are not necessarily measurable outcomes because many memes do not convey factual information—or even opinions, at times. Instead, as our baseline results suggest (and as implied by theory and analysis of Russian intent), a meme acts on viewers' emotions, and those emotions in turn are affected by viewers' perceptions of the meme's source and intended purpose. Future research will need to assess more critically this relationship between emotional response and any subsequent change in audience attitudes.[4]

The research design used in this study provides a model for future research testing the impact of state sponsored propaganda and interventions designed to mitigate that impact. Specifically, this study exposed participants to Russian-authored social media memes and real and false news memes and asked participants to rate those memes on various indices to include emotional reactions and the intent to like or share the memes on Facebook. Their responses to these memes helped determine the impact of the media literacy interventions and the source labels. Now established, future research can use and even improve on this model to advance our understanding of adversary propaganda campaigns.

---

[4] More generally, our results show that findings from previous studies in the context of false headlines do not translate to the emotionally directed disinformation disseminated by Russian efforts. The reactions to false news headlines and to Russian disinformation were often in opposite directions. Therefore, future research needs to focus specifically on the mechanisms for partisan and emotionally directed disinformation efforts, distinct from false news headlines.

APPENDIX A

Memes Used in This Study

In this appendix, we provide the memes (Figures A.1–A.11) that we showed each group. All memes are available for review upon request.

Figure A.1
Control Memes

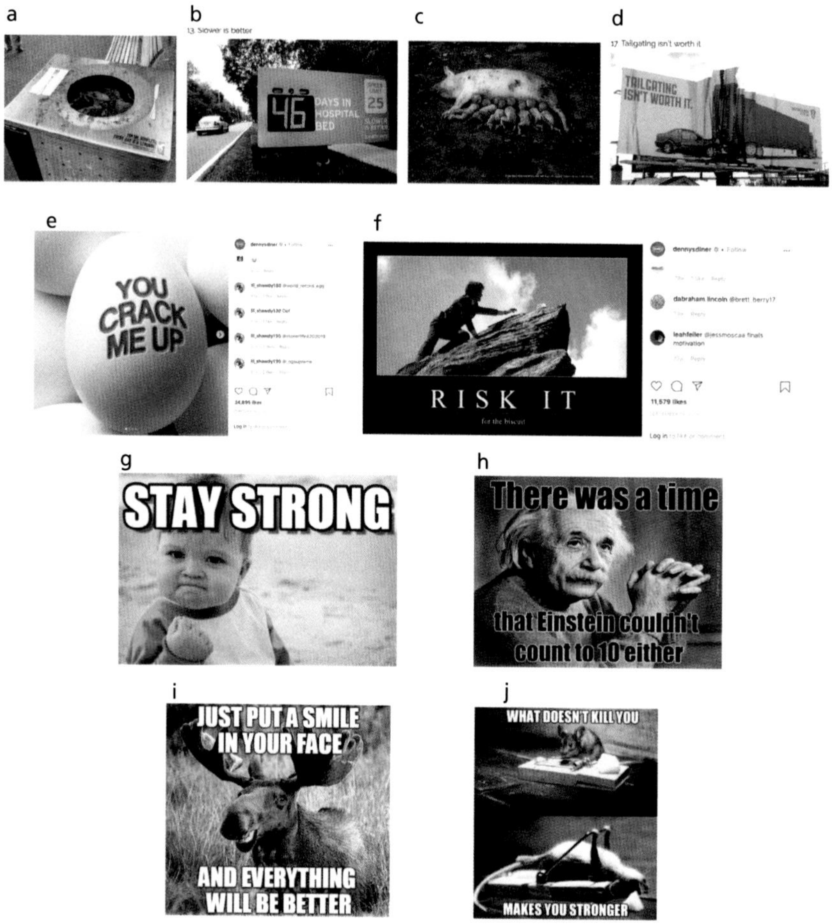

SOURCES: Images a–d: "60 Powerful Issue Ads . . .," undated; images e–f: Denny's restaurant chain Instagram account, undated; image g: SayingImages, undated; image h: Meme Generator, undated; image i: jokerry, undated; image j: alex19xd, undated.

For all conditions, we presented two memes that were advertisements from Denny's restaurant chain and two memes that were PSAs. Each participant was shown either two PSA memes with a hunger theme or two PSA memes with a "drive safely" theme. For the experimental groups that did not receive a media literacy intervention, we replaced two media literacy memes with two inspirational memes. To muddy the purpose of the study in the minds of participants, themes were presented in pairs: two media literacy or inspirational memes, plus two Denny's memes, plus two hunger or safe-driving memes.

Figure A.2
Media Literacy Memes

Use of highly emotional narratives or images often signal an attempt to manipulate. Stories, posts, images, or videos that make you feel outraged, scared, or really happy are designed to provoke a strong reaction. Take a deep breath, name the emotion you're feeling, and think about what the content creator might be trying to do, before you act.

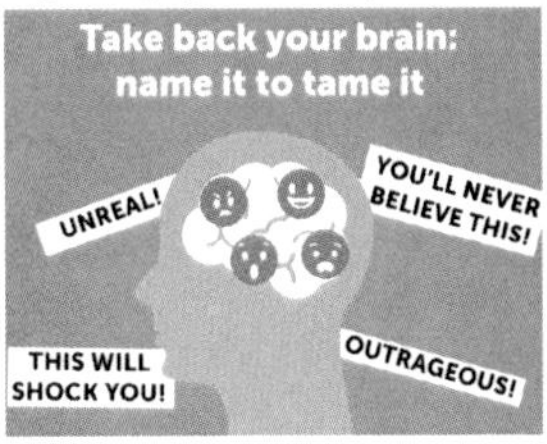

When you encounter a source that you're not sure can be trusted, check multiple sources to verify credibility. Advice from "a friend of a friend" or unspecified "experts" may not be reliable.

One of the best things you can do is limit your exposure to social media sites that push increasingly engaging content, which can quickly turn toxic. Turn off all but the most important notifications. Turn off autoplay on YouTube. Remove addictive apps from your phone. Resist clickbait. Stop scrolling and give your brain a break.

News that makes us feel good about our choices is attractive, but can leave us in a bubble of news that confirms what we want to hear. Diversify your information space to include credible, well-researched sources and evidence-based guidance.

Misinformation spreads easily online, confusing people about what actions to take and spreading panic. It's not always easy to tell at first glance whether information is reliable. Before you share information online, take 20 seconds to reflect on what you see.

It's good to take stock of how much social media you consume and set boundaries to avoid being influenced and overwhelmed. When we spend too much time online, we can sometimes lose perspective and are more vulnerable to manipulative information.

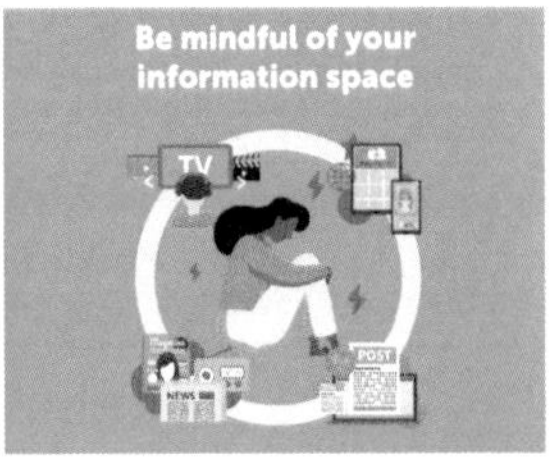

SOURCE: IREX, undated.
NOTE: Each participant was exposed to two memes randomly selected from this tranche of six memes focused on media literacy.

Figure A.3
Politically Right-Leaning Russian Memes Used as Part of the Disinformation Test Tranche

SOURCES: "When a Civilization . . .": IRACopyPasta asset rebel.va., (used and explained in François, Nimmo, and Eib, 2019); all others taken from U.S. House of Representatives Permanent Select Committee on Intelligence, 2015–2017.
NOTES: We used two Russian politically right-leaning memes as part of the disinformation test tranche. Each participant viewed one meme randomly selected from the anti-immigrant and pro-confederacy categories and one randomly selected meme from the gun-rights and religious categories.

Figure A.4
Politically Left-Leaning Russian Memes Used as Part of the Disinformation Test Tranche

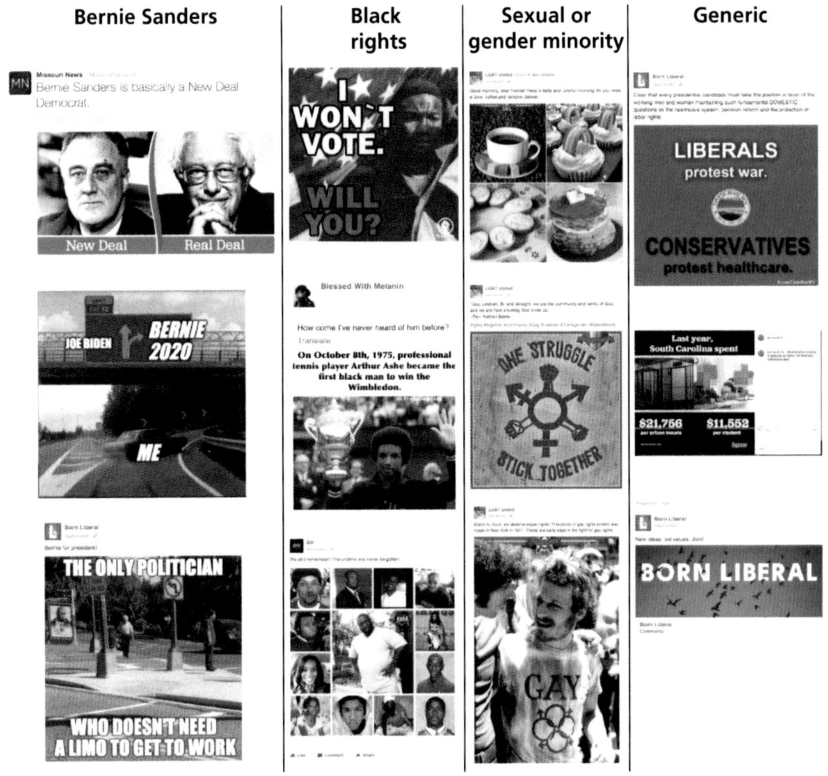

SOURCES: "Bernie 2020": Post by IRACopyPasta asset rebel.va., bernie.2020 (used in François, Nimmo, and Eib, 2019); "Last year, South Carolina spent…" Bernie Sanders, reposted by IRACopyPasta asset rebel.va., bernie.2020 (used in François, Nimmo, and Eib, 2019); all others image taken from U.S. House of Representatives Permanent Select Committee on Intelligence, 2015–2017.
NOTES: We used two Russian left-leaning memes as part of the disinformation test tranche. Each participant viewed one meme randomly selected from the Bernie Sanders and Black rights categories and one randomly selected meme from the gender minority and generic liberal group categories.

Figure A.5
Pro-U.S. Russian Memes Used as Part of the Disinformation Test Tranche

Veterans

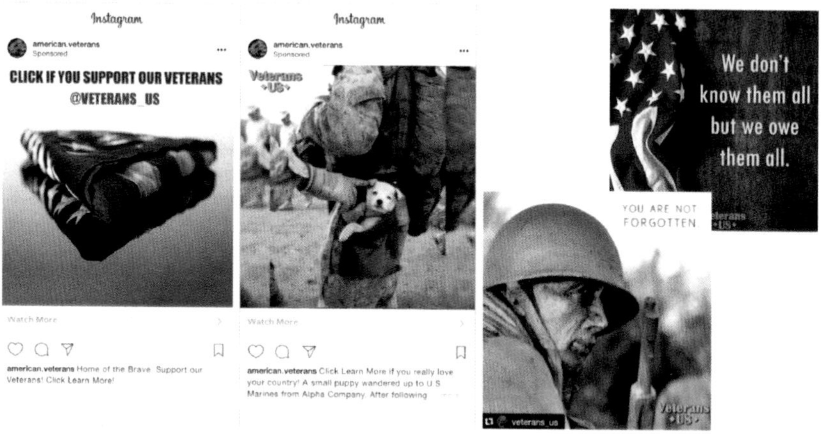

Patriotism

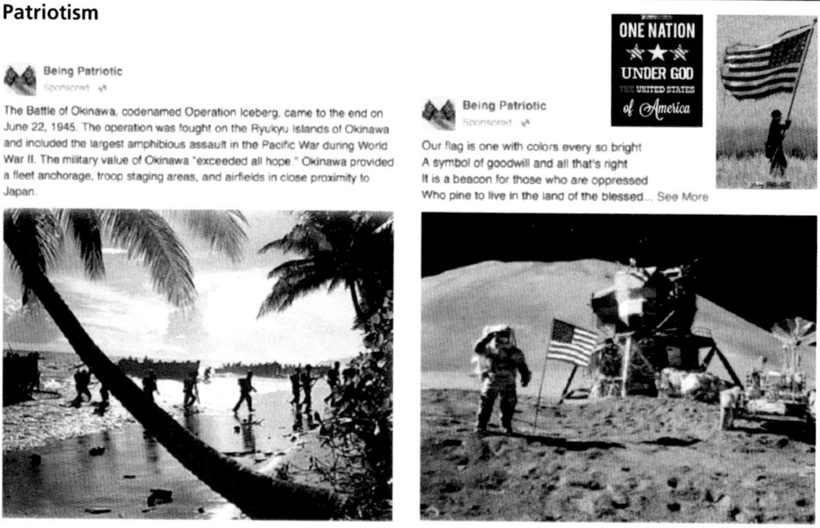

SOURCES: "We don't know them all": IRA watermarked meme posted by wisconsin.blue.family (used in François, Nimmo, and Eib, 2019); all others taken from U.S. House of Representatives Permanent Select Committee on Intelligence, 2015–2017.
NOTES: Each participant viewed one meme randomly selected from the veteran-related memes and one meme randomly selected from the pro-U.S. memes.

Figure A.6
COVID-19 False News Memes Used as Part of the Disinformation Test Tranche

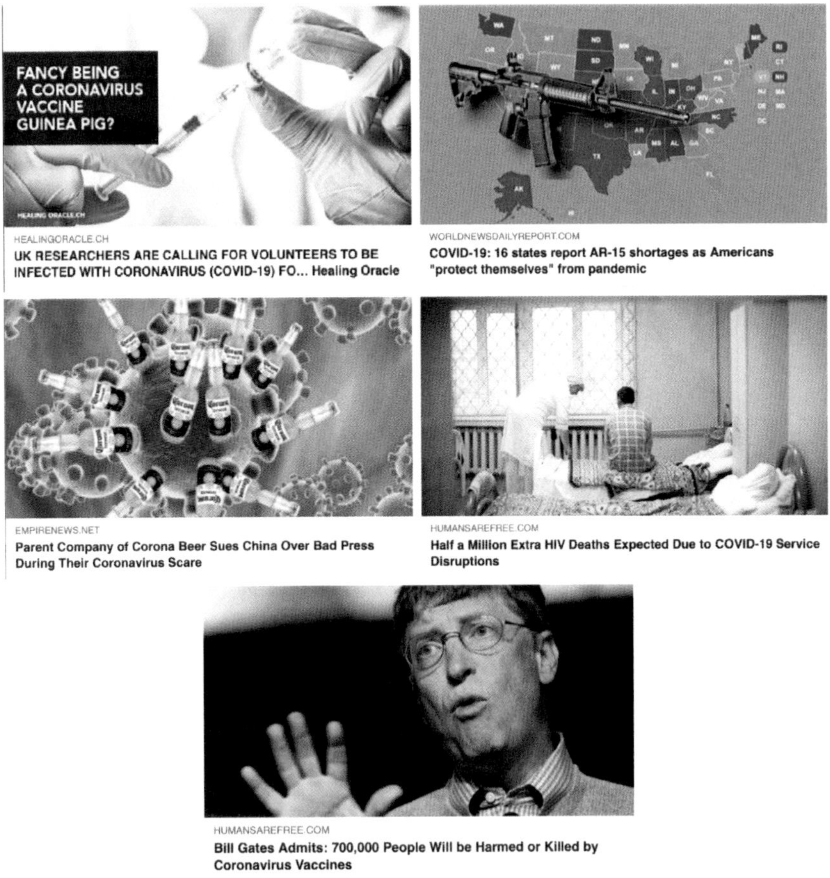

SOURCES: COVID-19 false news content: Empire News, undated; Healing Oracle, undated; and World News Daily Report, undated. Generic false news content: Humans Are Free, undated.
NOTES: Each participant viewed one meme randomly selected from the COVID-19 false news category. The sourcing descriptions we provided in our study read as follows: "*Source*: Empirenews.net is a false-news and satirical website." "*Source*: Healingoracle.ch, a website that disseminates false, misleading or unproven information." "*Source*: Worldnewsdailyreport.com, a false-news & satirical website." "Source: Humansarefree.com, a website that disseminates false, misleading or

Figure A.7
Generic False News Memes Used as Part of the Disinformation Test Tranche

SOURCE: World News Daily Report, undated.
NOTE: Each participant viewed one meme randomly selected from the generic false news category. The sourcing descriptions we provided in our study read as follows: "Source: Worldnewsdailyreport.com, a false-news & satirical website."

Figure A.8
Authentic COVID-19 News Memes Used as Part of the Disinformation Test Tranche

SOURCES: Associated Press, undated; PBS, undated.
NOTE: Each participant viewed one meme randomly selected from the genuine COVID news category. The sourcing descriptions we provided in our study read as follows: *"Source*: The Associated Press (AP), an American not-for-profit news agency." "Source: The Public Broadcasting Service is an American Public Broadcaster and Television Program Distributor."

Figure A.9
Authentic Generic News Memes Used as Part of the Disinformation Test Tranche

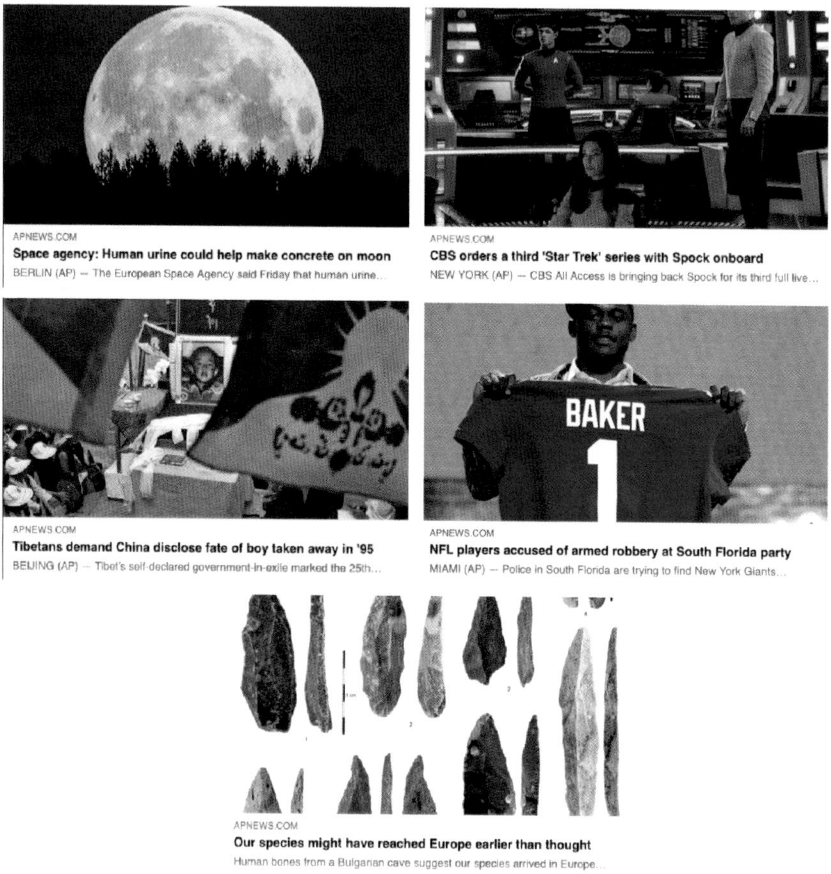

SOURCE: Associated Press, undated.
NOTE: Each participant viewed one meme randomly selected from the authentic generic news category.

Figure A.10
Public Service Announcements Used as Part of the Disinformation Test Tranche

SOURCE: "60 Powerful Issue Ads . . .," undated.
NOTES: Each participant viewed two randomly selected PSA memes. Sourcing descriptions provided to participants were as follows: (a) "*Source*: The Government of Alberta, Canada." (b) "*Source*: The United Kingdom's National Autism Society." (c) "*Source*: "Friends of the Earth, a U.S. nongovernmental environmental organization based in the U.S." (d) "*Source*: Australian Childhood Foundation, a not-for-profit organization dedicated to supporting children and families devastated by abuse, family violence, and neglect." (e) "*Source*: Ad promoting breast self-exams, created by the retail firm, Shopping Patio Dom Luis." (f) "*Source*: Czech Republic chapter of the International Federation of Red Cross and Red Crescent Societies, which is a worldwide humanitarian aid organization." (g) "*Source*: American Disability Association, a nonprofit 501(c)(3) organization supporting children with disabilities and their families." (h) "*Source*: CARA Welfare Philippines, an animal rescue organization." (i) "*Source*: Workers are Not Tools, an organization committed to increasing awareness of sweatshops and forced labor." (j) "*Source*: Coop Mútua-Acão is a Brazilian based cooperative that works on community social psychology issues."

Figure A.11
Examples of How the Source Information Was Paired with Memes as Part of the Conditions in Which the Meme Source Was Displayed

Source: The Russian government, which recently disseminated this and other social media memes as part of a covert propaganda campaign in the United States.

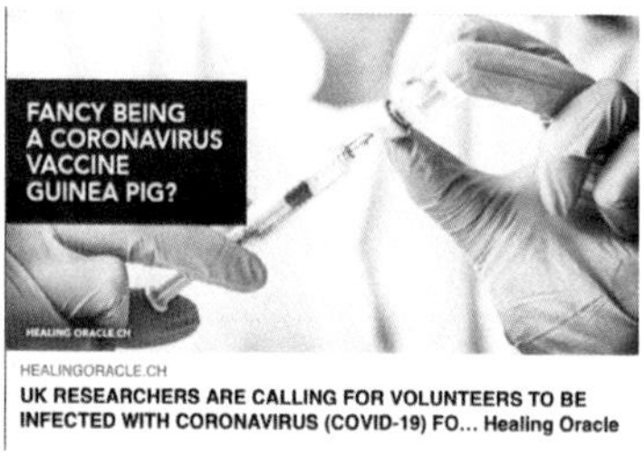

Source: Humansarefree.com, a website that disseminates false, misleading or unproven content.

APPENDIX B

Supplementary Results

Sample Balance and Power

The baseline sample was randomized to treatment groups using age, gender, state, and political beliefs. After attrition, the analytic sample that responded to Test Session 1 was distributed as follows: 398 participants (26 percent) in the control group, 401 (26 percent) in the "source revealed" group, 340 (22 percent) in the media literacy video group, and 390 (26 percent) in the media literacy meme group. To assess balance, we conducted a test of joint orthogonality by running a multinomial logit regression using all covariates in Table 3.3 and the 29 news sources (listed in Chapter Three; also see Figure B.1). The likelihood ratio chi-square statistic is 22.49 with a *p*-value of 0.80, indicating that the covariates are not jointly statistically significant in predicting treatment assignment.

In the two-way comparison between any treatment group and the control, given the sample size, a power analysis assuming 5-percent probability of Type I error and 20-percent probability of Type II error (i.e., 80-percent power) showed that the minimum detectable effect size would be at least 0.15, depending on the group being compared.[1]

[1] These power calculations are for the full-sample analyses. For subgroup analyses, the minimum detectable effect sizes are accordingly larger because the subsamples are smaller.

Latent Class Analyses

To identify the optimal number of latent classes for news consumption and emotional responses, we ran models with various numbers of classes and compared goodness-of-fit statistics. For each model, the set of categorical inputs consisted of binary indicators of whether a participant used a given news source or selected a given emotional reaction.

Figure B.1 shows the survey sample distribution of readership across the 29 news items.

We ran models with between two and nine classes, using 50 repetitions of each model to find the global maximum log-likelihood (results were not sensitive to any number of repetitions larger than 20).[2] For each model, we recorded three statistics (see Figure B.2): the Bayesian Information Criterion (BIC), the adjusted BIC (ABIC), and the asymptotically consistent Akaike Information Criterion (CAIC).

Simulation studies suggest that the BIC best identifies the optimal model (Nylund, Asparouhov, and Muthén, 2007).[3] In this case, the 6-class model has the minimum BIC, but difference in fit between the 5-class and 6-class is small and the CAIC implies the two are nearly equivalent.[4] Comparing the 5-class and 6-class models, we found that the "extra" sixth class consisted primarily of a combination of those in the *Partisan Left* with a few *Intuitive Omnivores* and *Disengaged Intuits*, with no clear conceptual identity of its own to distinguish it from the other classes. In addition, with just 61 people, we would not have been able to analyze this class separately. We also examined principal components and found that the additional explained variance leveled off once more than five factors were used. Finally, in ordinary least squares regressions of our outcome variables on the classes from the 5-class versus 6-class models, we found no difference in R-squared. We therefore opted to use the 5-class model.

---

2 We use the poLCA package in Linzer and Lewis, 2011.

3 This article also provides definitions of the statistics used here.

4 We ignored the ABIC because it achieved no minimum value and, as noted by Nylund, Asparouhov, and Muthén, 2007, it tends to point to too many classes when it fits poorly rather than too few.

Figure B.1
Survey Participants' Sources of News in Past Week

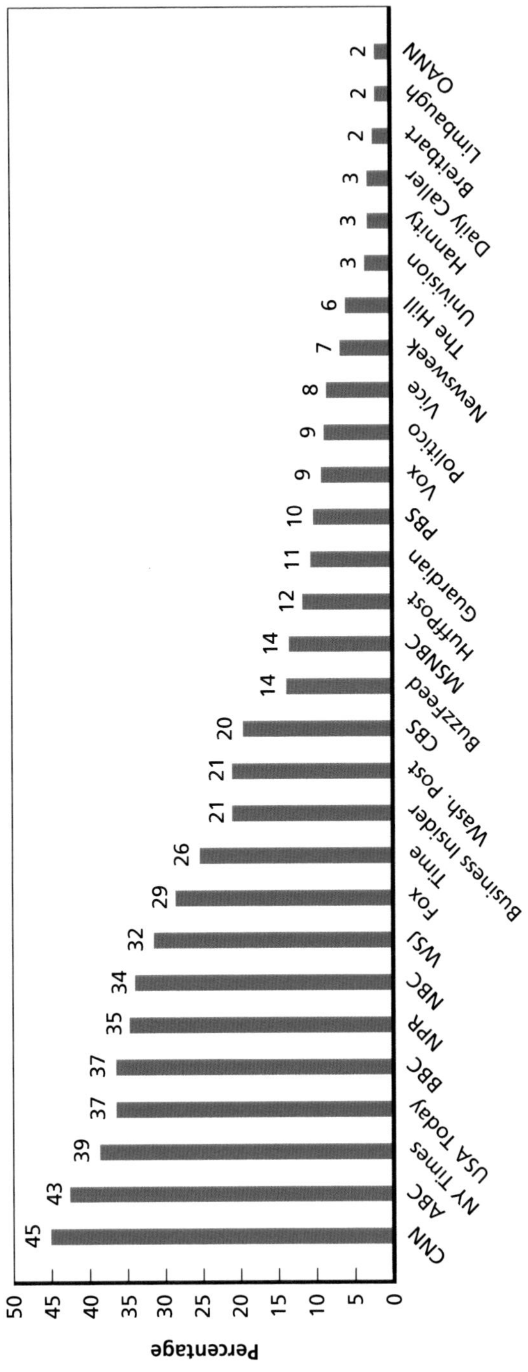

Figure B.2
Fit Statistics for Latent Class Models of News Consumption

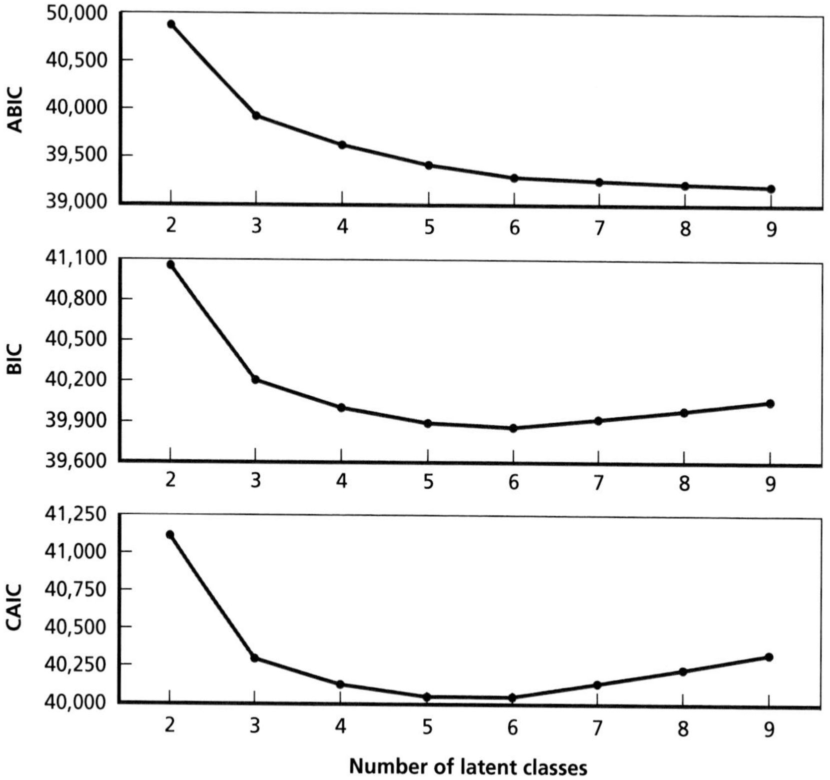

For each of the six types of test tranche content, we also ran latent class models for the nine emotions listed in the survey, comparing 2-, 3-, and 4-class models. In each case, the 2- or 3-class model had optimal fit. We opted to use the 2-class model in all cases for the sake of conformity and because of its simple conceptual distinction between "positive" and "negative" emotions.

When we examined the 3-class models, we found that they generally distinguished "positive" and "negative" emotions from feeling "fine" or "confused." Robustness checks show that there is no effect on our overall story if we instead use the 3-class models with a binary outcome variable indicating "positive response" as opposed to "fine/ confused" or "negative."

Pretest Content

Prior to calculating treatment effects we assessed participants' reactions to pretest content. If the experimental design is valid, participants who received no media literacy intervention should have the same reaction to each type of pretest content. In addition, if the media literacy memes do not change participants' views of nonpolitical content, then there should be no differences between the control and literacy meme treatment condition, either.

Table B.1 shows the mean for each outcome and the *p*-value from t-tests that each treatment group differs from the control. There are no substantial or significant differences between the control group and either of the two comparison treatment groups.

The media literacy memes mostly received similar average ratings. Two memes stood out with particularly high and low ratings, with correspondingly high or low fractions of the participants saying they would "like" it or share it. The highest rated was the "wash your hands" meme shown in Appendix A. This had an average rating of 3.76 out of 5, with 72 percent and 60 percent of participants saying they would "like" and share it, respectively. The lowest-rated meme was "take back your brain: name it to tame it," with an average rating of 3.43 out of 5 and 49 percent and 46 percent of participants saying they would "like" and share it.

Participants were randomly assigned pairs of literacy memes, and the highest- and lowest-rated memes belonged to separate pairs; thus, no one saw both. To check whether treatment effects differed by meme pair, we compared the emotional responses to different categories of test content using the media literacy memes participants saw during the pretest. We found no significantly different effects for the pairs with the highest- and lowest-rated memes compared with the third pair.

The media literacy video was rated higher than the other categories of pretest content, with an average of 4.0 out of 5. Sixty-six percent of participants said they would "like" the video on social media and 60 percent said they would share it. Participants were asked to state what they liked most and least about the video. Most often, participants said they liked the visuals and graphics or they felt the infor-

Table B.1
Reactions to Pretest Content, by Treatment Condition

	Control	Informed of Source		Media Literacy Meme	
Outcome	**Mean**	**Mean**	**[*p*-value]**	**Mean**	**[*p*-value]**
Like or dislike (5-point scale)					
Denny's ads	3.40	3.39	[0.91]	3.42	[0.69]
PSAs	3.26	3.19	[0.28]	3.32	[0.41]
Inspirational	3.70	3.60	[0.31]	—	—
Would "like"					
Denny's ads	0.50	0.48	[0.45]	0.50	[0.88]
PSAs	0.46	0.46	[0.78]	0.48	[0.28]
Inspirational	0.58	0.56	[0.26]	—	—
Would share					
Denny's ads	0.43	0.47	[0.19]	0.44	[0.70]
PSAs	0.42	0.42	[0.86]	0.47	[0.07]
Inspirational	0.51	0.51	[0.84]	—	—

NOTE: — indicates that this meme category was not shown to this particular participant group.

mation was new, relevant, or both. But the most commonly disliked aspects were that the video was too long, went too fast, or didn't offer enough specific actionable tips on how to respond to disinformation.

In summary, we cannot say to what degree the idiosyncratic features of our media literacy interventions explain the treatment effects (or lack thereof). We do not find evidence that effects depend on the set of literacy memes that a participant viewed. But feedback to the video shows that the efficacy of the intervention likely could be improved by editing the design, the content, or both.

Multiple-Hypothesis Testing

In analyses conducted separately by type of content, we checked the robustness of the results after adjusting for the multiple hypotheses being tested. We conducted joint tests and multiple hypothesis tests using the method described in Young, 2019. Throughout the report, we showed unadjusted 95-percent confidence intervals for marginal effects, and we reported in the test cases any relevant results of the multiple-hypothesis tests. Here, we show that the results do not depend on whether we show adjusted or unadjusted *p*-values.

Table B.2 reports the unadjusted *p*-values for the main analyses presented in the text alongside the randomization-*t* *p*-values from Young, 2019, and adjusted *p*-values for tests of overall significance using the step-down method of Westfall and Young (see Westfall and Young, 1993; and Young, 2019).[5] The Westfall and Young method has the same interpretation but yields more statistical power than the Bonferroni correction, another commonly used approach, because it accounts for the covariance between *p*-values. Young, 2019, implements the method using randomization inference; that is, by performing a simulation to uncover the distribution of test statistics given the experimental design. This helps to account for outlier observations. Because participants were randomized according to political belief, we expect each political subsample to be well balanced across treatment arms, meaning that the adjusted *p*-values

[5] We used the RANDCMD package in Stata (Young, 2020).

Table B.2
Adjusted *p*-Values from Multiple Hypothesis Testing

Outcome	Treatment	*p*-value	PSAs	False News	Real News	Left-Leaning Russian	Pro-U.S. Russian	Right-Leaning Russian
Positive response	Informed of source	Unadjusted	0.779	0.029	0.448	0.003	< 0.001	0.115
		Adjusted	0.769	0.027	0.439	0.005	0.001	0.113
	Literacy video	Unadjusted	0.703	0.538	0.054	0.470	0.650	0.719
		Adjusted	0.698	0.539	0.058	0.469	0.653	0.721
	Literacy memes	Unadjusted	0.452	0.074	0.940	0.107	0.817	0.262
		Adjusted	0.465	0.068	0.942	0.119	0.804	0.264
		Joint (randomization-*t*)	0.750	0.120	0.202	0.001	0.001	0.404
		Westfall and Young	0.811	0.072	0.143	0.012	0.001	0.270
		Westfall and Young (all parameters)	0.008					
Would "like"	Informed of source	Unadjusted	0.470	0.855	0.373	0.120	< 0.001	0.812
		Adjusted	0.471	0.873	0.361	0.118	0.001	0.808
	Literacy video	Unadjusted	0.698	0.267	0.686	0.895	0.030	0.219
		Adjusted	0.687	0.312	0.684	0.896	0.038	0.222
	Literacy memes	Unadjusted	0.572	0.519	0.500	0.074	0.565	0.260
		Adjusted	0.546	0.505	0.508	0.078	0.571	0.284
		Joint (randomization-*t*)	0.555	0.703	0.451	0.012	0.004	0.329
		Joint (Westfall and Young)	0.823	0.613	0.693	0.189	0.001	0.484
		Joint (all parameters)	0.008					

Table B.2—Continued

Outcome	Treatment	*p*-value	PSAs	False News	Real News	Left-Leaning Russian	Pro-U.S. Russian	Right-Leaning Russian
Would share	Informed of source	Unadjusted	0.447	0.201	0.160	0.183	0.817	0.257
		Adjusted	0.438	0.223	0.160	0.166	0.805	0.249
	Literacy video	Unadjusted	0.472	0.359	0.953	0.303	0.232	0.306
		Adjusted	0.468	0.384	0.943	0.288	0.246	0.297
	Literacy memes	Unadjusted	0.521	0.326	0.304	0.836	0.031	0.354
		Adjusted	0.547	0.333	0.335	0.843	0.023	0.352
		Joint (randomization-*t*)	0.434	0.148	0.125	0.466	0.050	0.113
		Joint (Westfall and Young)	0.782	0.477	0.354	0.369	0.057	0.518
		Joint (all parameters)	0.309					

NOTES: This table shows unadjusted and adjusted *p*-values for full-sample analyses. Unadjusted values correspond to results shown in Figures 4.4 and 5.2. Adjusted *p*-values for individual treatment effects are randomization-*t* *p*-values from the method of Young, 2019. Joint tests of the three treatment effects for each group of content are calculated according to Young, 2019, and Westfall and Young,1993. For each outcome, the joint test across all types of content of all 18 treatment effects is calculated according to Westfall and Young, 1993.

for our main analysis (particularly Figure 4.3) are less likely to diverge from the unadjusted *p*-values than if we had not randomized on political belief.[6] Joint tests were conducted for each group of content and for the 18 treatment effects as a whole. For the sake of space, only the results for the full sample are shown. When an adjusted *p*-value differed in a relevant way for any subgroup analysis, we note as much in the main text.

---

6 See the related discussion in Young, 2019, pp. 595–596.

References

"60 Powerful Issue Ads That'll Make You Stop and Think," Digital Synopsis, undated. As of August 12, 2020:
https://digitalsynopsis.com/inspiration/60-public-service-announcements-social-issue-ads

alex19xd, "What Doesn't Kill You Makes You Stronger! :d Mouse Version. :)," Meme Center, undated. As of September 25, 2020:
https://www.memecenter.com/fun/2375411/what-doesn-amp-039-t-kill-you-makes-you-stronger-d-mouse-version

Alvarez, German, Jaewon Royce Choi, and Sharon Strover, "Good News, Bad News: A Sentiment Analysis of the 2016 Election Russian Facebook Ads," *International Journal of Communication*, Vol. 14, 2020, pp. 3027–3053.

Associated Press, homepage, undated. As of September 20, 2020:
https://apnews.com

Bail, Christopher A., Brian Guay, Emily Maloney, Aidan Combs, D. Sunshine Hillygus, Friedolin Merhout, Deen Freelon, and Alexander Volfovsky, "Assessing the Russian Internet Research Agency's Impact on the Political Attitudes and Behaviors of American Twitter Users in Late 2017," *Proceedings of the National Academy of Sciences*, Vol. 117, No. 1, 2020, pp. 243–250.

Bakshy, Eytan, Solomon Messing, and Lada A. Adamic, "Exposure to Ideologically Diverse News and Opinion on Facebook," *Science*, Vol. 348, No. 6239, 2015, pp. 1130–1132.

Banas, John A., and Gregory Miller, "Inducing Resistance to Conspiracy Theory Propaganda: Testing Inoculation and Metainoculation Strategies," *Human Communication Research*, Vol. 39, No. 2, 2013, pp. 184–207.

Barberá, Pablo, "How Social Media Reduces Mass Political Polarization: Evidence from Germany, Spain, and the U.S.," Working Paper, University of Southern California, 2015.

Berger, Jonah, and Katherine L. Milkman, "What Makes Online Content Viral?" *Journal of Marketing Research*, Vol. 49, No. 2, 2012, pp. 192–205.

Braddock, Kurt, "Vaccinating Against Hate: Using Attitudinal Inoculation to Confer Resistance to Persuasion by Extremist Propaganda," *Terrorism and Political Violence*, November 2019.

Chotikul, Diane, *The Soviet Theory of Reflexive Control in Historical and Psychocultural Perspective: A Preliminary Study*, Monterey, Calif.: Naval Postgraduate School, No. NPS55-86-013, 1986.

Clayton, Katherine, Spencer Blair, Jonathan A. Busam, Samuel Forstner, John Glance, Guy Green, Anna Kawata, Akhila Kovvuri, Jonathan Martin, Evan Morgan, Morgan Sandhu, Rachel Sang, Rachel Scholz-Bright, Austin T. Welch, Andrew G. Wolff, Amanda Zhou, and Brendan Nyhan, "Real Solutions for Fake News? Measuring the Effectiveness of General Warnings and Fact-Check Tags in Reducing False Stories on Social Media," *Political Behavior*, February 2019.

Computational Propaganda Research Project, *The IRA, Social Media and Political Polarization in the United States, 2012–2018*, 2018.

Constine, Josh, "Facebook Puts Link to 10 Tips for Spotting 'False News' Atop Feed," Techcrunch, April 6, 2017. As of August 21, 2020:
https://techcrunch.com/2017/04/06/
facebook-puts-link-to-10-tips-for-spotting-false-news-atop-feed/

Cook, John, Stephan Lewandowsky, and Ullrich K. H. Ecker, "Neutralizing Misinformation Through Inoculation: Exposing Misleading Argumentation Techniques Reduces Their Influence," *PLoS One*, Vol. 12, No. 5, 2017.

Dawkins, Richard, *The Selfish Gene*, Oxford, UK: Oxford University Press, 1976.

Denny's, @dennysdiner, Instagram, undated. As of October 1, 2020:
https://www.instagram.com/dennysdiner/?hl=en

DiResta, Renee, Kris Shaffer, Becky Ruppel, David Sullivan, Robert Matney, Ryan Fox, Jonathan Albright, and Ben Johnson, *The Tactics and Tropes of the Internet Research Agency*, New Knowledge, 2019.

Empire News, homepage, undated. As of September 25, 2020:
https://empirenews.net

François, Camile, Ben Nimmo, and C. Shawn Eib, *The IRACopyPasta Campaign*, Graphika, October 21, 2019. As of August 30, 2020:
https://public-assets.graphika.com/reports/graphika_report_copypasta.pdf

Frederick, Shane, "Cognitive Reflection and Decision Making," *Journal of Economic Perspectives*, Vol. 19, No. 4, 2005, pp. 25–42.

Greene, Steven, "The Social-Psychological Measurement of Partisanship," *Political Behavior*, Vol. 24, No. 3, 2002, pp. 171–197.

Guess, Andrew M., Michael Lerner, Benjamin Lyons, Jacob M. Montgomery, Brendan Nyhan, Jason Reifler, and Neelanjan Sircar, "A Digital Media Literacy Intervention Increases Discernment Between Mainstream and False News in the United States and India," *PNAS*, Vol. 117, No. 27, 2020, pp. 15536–15545.

Guess, Andrew M., Brendan Nyhan, and Jason Reifler, "Exposure to Untrustworthy Websites in the 2016 US Election," *Nature Human Behavior*, Vol. 4, 2020, pp. 472–480.

Healing Oracle, homepage, undated. As of September 25, 2020: https://healingoracle.ch

Hugh, Brigitte, and Anna O. Pechenkina, *Positive Messaging in the 2016 Russian Online Manipulation Campaign*, Logan, Utah: Utah State University, unpublished report, April 20, 2020.

Humans Are Free, homepage, undated. As of September, 22, 2020: https://humansarefree.com

IREX, homepage, undated. As of August 25, 2020: https://www.irex.org

Isaac, Mike and Daisuke Wakabayashi, "Russian Influence Reached 126 Million Through Facebook Alone," New York Times, October 30, 2017.

Jeong, Se-Hoon, Hyunyi Cho, and Yoori Hwang, "Media Literacy Interventions: A Meta-Analytic Review," *Journal of Communication*, Vol. 62, No. 3, 2012, pp. 454–472.

jokerry, "91 Funny Inspirational Memes for Those [Who] Are Seeking Motivation," Pinterest, undated. As of September 25, 2020: https://www.pinterest.com/pin/348536458662286914/?nic_v2=1a4YKo59q

Lefebvre, Vladimir A., "The Elements of Reflexive Game Logic," Problems in Engineering Psychology, No. 4, 1966.

Linvill, Daren L., Brandon C. Boatwright, Will J. Grant, and Patrick L. Warren, "'The Russians Are Hacking My Brain!' Investigating Russia's Internet Research Agency Twitter Tactics During the 2016 United States Presidential Campaign," *Computers in Human Behavior*, Vol. 99, 2019, pp. 292–300.

Linzer, Drew A., and Jeffrey B. Lewis, "poLCA: An R Package for Polytomous Latent Class Analysis," *Journal of Statistical Software*, Vol. 42, No. 10, 2011, pp. 1–29.

Maksl, Adam, Seth Ashley, and Stephanie Craft, "Measuring News Media Literacy," *Journal of Media Literacy Education,* Vol. 6, No. 3, 2015, pp. 29–45.

Marcellino, William M., Christian Johnson, Marek N. Posard, and Todd C. Helmus, *Foreign Interference in the 2020 Election: Tools for Detecting Online Election Interference*, Santa Monica, Calif.: RAND Corporation, RR-A704-2, 2020. As of October 10, 2020:
https://www.rand.org/pubs/research_reports/RRA704-2.html

McCrae, James, "Meme Marketing: How Brands are Speaking a New Consumer Language," *Forbes*, May 8, 2017. As of August 20, 2020:
https://www.forbes.com/sites/forbescommunicationscouncil/2017/05/08/meme-marketing-how-brands-are-speaking-a-new-consumer-language

Meme Generator, "Einstein," undated. As of September 25, 2020:
https://memegenerator.net/instance/54608557

Nylund, Karen L., Tihomir Asparouhov, and Bengt O. Muthén, "Deciding on the Number of Classes in Latent Class Analysis and Growth Mixture Modeling: A Monte Carlo Simulation Study," *Structural Equation Modeling*, Vol. 14, No. 4, 2007, pp. 535–569.

Office of Nevada Secretary of State, "Voter Registration Statistics," January 2020. As of September 8, 2020:
https://www.nvsos.gov/sos/home/showdocument?id=8344

PBS, homepage, undated. As of September 20, 2020:
https://www.pbs.org

Pennycook, Gordon, Adam Bear, Evan T. Collins, and David G. Rand, "The Implied Truth Effect: Attaching Warnings to a Subset of Fake News Headlines Increases Perceived Accuracy of Headlines Without Warnings," *Management Science*, February 21, 2020, pp. 1–14.

Pennycook, Gordon, and David G. Rand, "Lazy, Not Biased: Susceptibility to Partisan Fake News Is Better Explained by Lack of Reasoning Than by Motivated Reasoning," *Cognition*, Vol. 188, 2019, pp. 39–50.

Posard, Marek N., Marta Kepe, Hilary Reininger, James V. Marrone, Todd C. Helmus, and Jordan R. Reimer, *From Consensus to Conflict: Understanding Foreign Measures Targeting U.S. Elections*, Santa Monica, Calif.: RAND Corporation, RR-A704-1, 2020. As of October 1, 2020:
https://www.rand.org/pubs/research_reports/RRA704-1.html

Public Policy Institute of California, "California's Population," webpage, April 2020a. As of September 5, 2020:
https://www.ppic.org/publication/californias-population/

———, "California Voter and Party Profiles," webpage, September 2020b. As of September 24, 2020:
https://www.ppic.org/publication/california-voter-and-party-profiles/

Radin, Andrew, Alyssa Demus, and Krystyna Marcinek, *Understanding Russian Subversion: Patterns, Threats, and Responses*, Santa Monica, Calif.: RAND Corporation, PE-331-A, 2020. As of July 14, 2020: https://www.rand.org/pubs/perspectives/PE331.html

RAND Corporation, "Tools that Fight Disinformation Online," webpage, undated. As of September 5, 2020: https://www.rand.org/research/projects/truth-decay/fighting-disinformation/search.html

Ribeiro, Filipe N., Koustuv Saha, Mahmoudreza Babaei, Lucas Henrique, Johnnatan Messias, Fabricio Benevenuto, Oana Goga, Krishna P. Gummadi, and Elissa M. Redmiles, "On Microtargeting Socially Divisive Ads: A Case Study of Russia-Linked Ad Campaigns on Facebook," *Proceedings on the ACM Conference on Fairness, Accountability, and Transparency*, Association for Computing Machinery, January 2019, pp. 140–149.

SayingImages, "Be Strong Meme Baby Fist," undated. As of September 25, 2020: https://sayingimages.com/be-strong-meme-baby-fist/

Secretary of State, State of Arizona, "Voter Registration & Historical Election Data," webpage, undated. As of September 8, 2020: https://azsos.gov/elections/voter-registration-historical-election-data

Stewart, Leo G., Ahmer Arif, and Kate Starbird, *Examining Trolls and Polarization with a Retweet Network*, Seattle: University of Washington, MIS2, 2018.

Thomas, Timothy L., "Russia's Reflexive Control Theory and the Military," *Journal of Slavic Military Studies*, Vol. 17, 2004, pp. 237–256.

Tripodi, Francesca, Searching for Alternative Facts: Analyzing Scriptural Inference in Conservative News Practices, New York: Data and Society Research Institute, 2018.

Tucker, Joshua A., Andrew Guess, Pablo Barberá, Cristian Vaccari, Alexandra Siegel, Sergey Sanovich, Denis Stukal, and Brendan Nyhan, *Social Media, Political Polarization, and Political Disinformation: A Review of the Scientific Literature*, Menlo Park, Calif.: Hewlett Foundation, March 2018.

U.S. House of Representatives Permanent Select Committee on Intelligence, "Social Media Advertisements," webpage, 2015–2017 (assorted). As of August 30, 2020: https://intelligence.house.gov/social-media-content/social-media-advertisements.htm

van der Linden, Sander, Edward Maibach, John Cook, Anthony Leiserowitz, and Stephan Lewandowsky, "Inoculating Against Misinformation," *Science*, Vol. 358, No. 6367, 2017, pp. 1141–1142.

van Prooijen, Jan-Willem, André P. M. Krouwel, and Thomas V. Pollet, "Political Extremism Predicts Belief in Conspiracy Theories," *Social Psychology and Personality Science*, Vol. 6, No. 5, 2015, pp. 570–578.

Westfall, Peter H., and S. Stanley Young, *Resampling-Based Multiple Testing: Examples and Methods for p-Value Adjustment*, New York: John Wiley & Sons, 1993.

World News Daily Report, homepage, undated. As of September 20, 2020: https://worldnewsdailyreport.com

Xu, Qian, "Dual Process Models of Persuasion," in Patrick Rössler, Cynthia A. Hoffner, and Liesbet van Zoonen, eds., *The International Encyclopedia of Media Effects*, West Sussex, UK: Wiley-Blackwell, 2017, pp. 1–13.

Young, Alwyn, "Channeling Fisher: Randomization Tests and the Statistical Significance of Seemingly Significant Experimental Results," *Quarterly Journal of Economics*, Vol. 134, No. 2, 2019, pp. 557–598.

Young, Alwyn, "RANDCMD: Stata Module to Compute Randomization Inference p-Values," Statistical Software Components, S458774, Boston College Department of Economics, 2020.